*The Alien Protagonist of* FORD MADOX FORD

*The Alien Protagonist of FORD MADOX FORD*

*by H. Robert Huntley*

*The University of North Carolina Press · Chapel Hill*

*For my mother and father*

# Preface

Some eight years ago a kindly professor cautioned me against devoting any serious or protracted attention to Ford Madox Ford. Although Ford criticism was the merest trickle at the time, he saw that the floodgates were about to open; and subsequent events have proven the accuracy of his prediction. This volume, however, represents my own reluctance to abandon a writer whose versatility and sometime genius I once ingenuously regarded as my private discovery.

Although this study is aimed at the general reader as well as the more specialized student of Ford, its emphasis quite obviously differs from that of most other recent studies. The majority of these have been obliged to deal with the entire body of Ford's work, placing both his fiction and his nonfiction within the context of his personal development as well as developments in the form of the novel itself, especially during the crucial Edwardian years. Because so much of the critical landscape has been cleared, it has only recently become possible to concentrate on more specialized problems, as I have attempted to do.

This book focuses on the problem of that oft-noted similarity between so many of Ford's protagonists, men whose peculiarly alien temperaments and ethics lead them into inevitable conflict with their particular milieu. The central argument of the book is that behind these struggles, traced out through four successive centuries, lies a consciously contrived theory of historical and psychological evolution in the Western world. This *sub rosa* theory Ford used as an artistic construct in framing that conflict of ethical values waged unsuccessfully by his alien protagonists against their respective societies.

The aid and encouragement of more people than I can enumerate here lie behind this work. My foremost obligation is to Paul Wiley of the University of Wisconsin under whom I once had the good fortune to study and under whom I wrote a dissertation on Ford, which was in part the genesis of this book. To my own university I am indebted both for generous financial assistance and a year's leave of absence. And special thanks are due the staff of McCormick Library, who answered requests for books not available in the general Ford collection. Finally I wish to acknowledge my thanks to the Cooperative Program in the Humanities, administered by the University of North Carolina and Duke University, for a fellowship that provided the time, money, and surroundings which permitted the completion of this work.

H. R. H.

*Washington and Lee University*
*February, 1969*

# Contents

*The Alien Protagonist of* FORD MADOX FORD

# 1. The Mundane Cosmogony

> *"The actual universe is a thing wide open,
> but rationalism makes systems and systems
> must be closed."*
>
> WILLIAM JAMES

That intriguing similarity between so many of Ford Madox Ford's ill-starred protagonists has long since alerted critics to the possibility of some underlying "system" in Ford's fictional universe. The danger in such system-searching is both obvious and endemic: the logical—and therefore simplistic—reduction of the artist's work to some philosophic system at which he presumably arrived intellectually and thereafter consciously wove into the warp and woof of his art. Or, to put it most bluntly, as critics we tend to underestimate the degree to which the artist relies upon hunch and instinct. Ford, however, from both personal and artistic need, did attempt to impose a discernible pattern—what he once called his "private and particular image"—upon that "wide open" universe of which William James wrote. Consequently, while heeding James's warning against closed systems, the critic must nevertheless take his own lead from the philosopher's novelist brother, Henry, who urged the critic "to seek out some key" to the novelist's characteristic mode, "some utterance of his literary convictions, some indication of his ruling theory." More perhaps than with any of his contemporaries, there is in Ford just such a demonstrable connection between a "ruling theory" and a "literary conviction."

Early scholarship denied the existence of any pattern whatsoever in Ford's fiction, culminating in Hugh Kenner's summary dismissal: "Ford had no 'philosophy.' " [1] Whatever reservations were intended by the qualifying quotation marks, if Kenner was implying the nonexistence of any formal system of thought his statement was just, if unnecessary. Logic and dialectic are so obviously not the artist's tools, it seems gratuitous to have to point the fact out. If, on the other hand, Kenner was denying the existence of any comprehensive pattern in Ford's understanding and depiction of his age, he has made an egregious error. There is a readily discernible pattern in the conflicts of all Ford's earlier novels, a conflict between character and social milieu based on a deeply personal historical mythos. The situational conflicts of these early novels bear witness to a concept of historical movement Ford had clearly articulated in his earliest nonfictional writing.

In these works as well as in the novels one finds the "key" of which James wrote, and it is a key to the recurrent pattern of conflict that envelops nearly all of Ford's protagonists. Previous criticism has gone astray in suggesting a temperamental or psychological kinship between Ford's various heroes. Thus MacShane, who early glimpsed a sameness about Ford's ill-fated protagonists, argued that one sees "a distinct pattern of behavior and definite ethical canons" behind their actions; that they are all "altruists—living by a strict morality that is literally based upon Christian teachings. By pursuing this romantic ideal, they invariably end their careers either

1. Hugh Kenner, "Conrad and Ford: The Artistic Conscience," *Shenandoah*, III (Summer, 1952), 53.

in disaster . . . or by retiring for solace into the depths of the country."[2] Undeniably one can see a strain of altruism in many of Ford's protagonists. Katherine Howard, George Moffatt, Don Kelleg, Ashburnham, and Tietjens all have a touch of it, yet it is not this which solely distinguishes any one of them. Katherine Howard, in a moment of anger, is capable of perfectly unaltruistic violence in beating a servant. Nor can Ashburnham's sentimental philandering be called the result of "strict morality literally based upon Christian teachings," any more than the hard-headed skepticism of Edward Colman in *The "Half-Moon."*

Morton Dauwen Zabel felt the lowest common denominator among these strikingly similar figures was their mutual involvement in the problem of private honor and public necessity: "He [Ford] could locate the . . . problem of honor in history—the Katherine Howard trilogy or *Ladies Whose Bright Eyes*—and find an original means to define it there. He could define it even better in his own age—in *The Good Soldier* and the Tietjens series. . . ."[3] Again, an important element of honor is undoubtedly present in nearly all of these protagonists, but Ford never fails to suggest the Quixotic nature of that honor and the harm it can bring the innocent. And to use Zabel's own example, Katherine Howard at the end of both the first and second book of the trilogy simply surrenders to the pressures of the moment. The "original means" Ford used in dramatizing this problem, as Zabel puts it, is never explained or clarified.

The first book-length study of Ford, Richard Cassell's *Ford Madox Ford: A Study of His Novels*, largely follows Zabel in tracing the evolution of Ford's "gentleman of honor," those figures who epitomize "the individual conscience battling against itself and against society," though shortly later they are said to be "dedicated to the preservation of established society."[4] The apparent ambiguity

2. Frank MacShane, *New Republic*, CXXXII (April 4, 1955), 16–17.
3. Morton Dauwen Zabel, *Craft and Character* (New York, 1957), p. 260.
4. Richard A. Cassell, *Ford Madox Ford: A Study of His Novels* (Baltimore, 1961), pp. 114–15.

here lies not with Ford but with the critics who, in pursuit of larger game and contending with more general matters, have brushed by this point, despite the fact that it embodies the nucleus of Ford's artistic and thematic development. Occasionally this failure has resulted in serious misreading both of the novels and of Ford's intent. John Meixner, for example, argues the close resemblance of the character Blood in *Mr. Fleight* with Christopher Tietjens of *Parade's End*. Both are said to be landed aristocrats who, because of personal misoneism, have withdrawn from the disgusting spectacle presented by modern life. Though a superficial resemblance between Blood and Tietjens may be argued, the novels make it quite clear how they differ. Tietjens, the eighteenth-century Tory, has lost his way in a world where ethical concerns have ceased to matter and subsequently retreats to a green shade. Blood, by contrast, has chosen to remain within the world, cynically exploiting what he regards as a disintegrating society. Like a character out of Huxley, he feeds on the very object of his contempt, creating a cult of his own nausea; but he hardly resembles Christopher Tietjens.

A more complex approach to the problem of Ford's protagonists is taken by Norman Leer in *The Limited Hero in the Novels of Ford Madox Ford*. A good antidote to earlier studies, which have tended to sentimentalize Ford's protagonists, the study is, perhaps, too pejorative in its revisionism. And occasional ambiguities result from the proliferation of Ford's heroes into good heroes, bad heroes, and limited heroes. The limited heroes, Leer's main concern, are said to have retreated from the world and their responsibilities, selfishly hugging their private idealisms to their respective bosoms. The result is a continuing collapse of Western civilization. Such a reading is only possible if one works from the novels alone, ignoring Ford's writings on the movement of history. But to do this results in making Ford's protagonists more responsible for their own fate than they actually are. And it also overlooks Ford's frequent references in his critical writings to the role of destiny, "august and inscrutable," which should figure as causation in all narrative.

Probably the most typical approach to the Fordian hero is that exemplified by R. W. Lid in *Ford Madox Ford: The Essence of His Art.* Working backwards and forwards from the Tietjens and Ashburnham figures, Lid extrapolates what he calls "Ford's typical gentleman of honor who ruins his life and the lives of the people he cares about." [5] Again, there is some merit in Lid's observation; but the word "honor," as Falstaff well knew, is a shadowy and ambiguous thing. And this is even more the case when it is used as a catchall for that surprisingly diverse band of heroes, drawn from four different centuries, each characterized by its own distinctive notion of appropriate human behavior.

As I have said, criticism has largely erred on this point by assuming some sort of temperamental affinity between Ford's protagonists. The affinity is there, but it is not, as most have suggested, a psychological one; it is rather a situational resemblance, one that has blinded us to the very real differences of personality among these various protagonists. All they really have in common is that each somehow fails to come to terms with his society, whether it is of the sixteenth or the twentieth century. When such persistent failure becomes the dominant motif in a novelist, the critic must ask himself whether the cause lies in some recurrent thematic technique or with some prevailing attitude on the part of the author. As with all such questions both possibilities play a part. There is a persistent theme running throughout the early novels, but it has its roots in Ford's personal view of Western civilization, and more specifically in his understanding of the movement of English history. The source of this view was not idiosyncratic but part of that common stock of late Victorian and Edwardian intellectual thought. Still there are specific sources in Ford's personal background that can be singled out to show how his personal understanding of these social forces was formed. And it is also true that the history of Ford's artistic develop-

5. Richard W. Lid, *Ford Madox Ford: The Essence of His Art* (Berkeley, Calif., 1964), p. 125.

ment is also a history of his attempt to incorporate implicitly in his art his diagnosis of his society according to that same historical movement.

Ford consistently proclaimed that the novel, as a form, could be a major cultural force by informing and reshaping public attitudes, that in its pages the concerned novelist might give his age some sense of where it stood in the long sweep of history by mirroring it against the perspective of its own historical past. In short, Ford's task as he conceived it was to show the Englishman what he had been and what he was now becoming. To accomplish this Ford sought for some satiric counter, some alien personality, with which to contrast the collective psychology of the Edwardian scene. It is this alien protagonist, and the struggle in which he is engaged, that provides the key to that curious similarity in the situations and fate of Ford's generous natures who always fall on evil times.

The word "protagonist" must be used here in a qualified sense, really for want of a more definitive term. Though these are the characters who most evoke the reader's sympathy and respect, as Ford intended, they cannot always be said to be the chief characters in the novels. Consequently, characters like Edward Ashburnham or Katherine Howard are not so much heroes and heroines as they are advocates or exemplars for past historical values in conflict with the social forces of their day, these social forces being the real focus of Ford's concern. For one to understand Ford's analysis of these forces it is necessary to recall briefly the milieu just preceding the Edwardian Age, for it was this that shaped both Ford's general view of history as well as his understanding of the mechanics upon which historical movement itself was generally thought to be based.

With uncharacteristic vagueness H. G. Wells, in his *Experiment in Autobiography*, could do no better than present a visual analogy in summarizing his impressions of Ford: "Ford is a long blond with a drawling manner, the very spit of his brother Oliver, and oddly resembling George Moore the novelist in pose and person. What he is really or if he is really, nobody knows now and he least of all; he has become a great system of assumed *personas* and dramatized selves." [6] There was the same haziness of outline in James's description of Ford as Merton Densher in *The Wings of the Dove*. Whatever this lifelong characteristic may or may not have betokened about Ford's personality, it is somehow appropriate for a writer who first came on the literary scene in the waning years of the Victorian Age.

Obviously no age is free of enigma, paradox, and downright self-contradiction, but none holds more fascination or frustration for the cultural historian than late-Victorian and Edwardian England. Gifted with more shapes than Proteus, it defies every attempt at oversimplification, and the dominant error both of history and of literary historians has been too often to accept at face value the contemporary voices of its most colorful and vocal figures. And yet if Wilde, Beardsley, and Dowson seem to suggest a pattern, Henley, Wells, and Kipling are there to contradict it; for Heroic Vitalism and Aestheticism were both on the scene, the fatal languor of the one always driving the other to an even more strident ebullience. Behind those dual notes of hope and despair lies one of the most interesting aspects of the age: the side-by-side existence of an Alpha and Omega complex—that bitterly disputed question of whether the age was winding down to extinction or on the verge of some brave new world.

Ford's own dark view of history derived from that general mood of decline that found its final requiem in Spengler's *The Decline of the West* many years later. But both this mood and the muscular optimism of the Vitalists, which Ford categorically opposed, had their common roots in Darwinian controversy, a controversy that implanted the notion of "process" indelibly on the Western mind, while leaving it free to interpret the end of that process as either promise or threat for the well-being of mankind. Darwin himself had seemed to suggest that natural selection itself promised an

6. H. G. Wells, *Experiment in Autobiography* (New York, 1934), p. 526.

improving lot for man: "We may look forward with some confidence to a secure future of great length. And as natural selection worked solely by and for the good of each being, all corporeal and mental endowments will tend to progress towards perfection." [7] It was inevitable that the advocates of Progress should in time turn to Darwin's doctrines as authority for their own roseate hopes for the future, though it was Herbert Spencer's *Synthetic Philosophy* that really hastened that gimcrack vision on its way. The distortion and oversimplification of Darwinian thought, gradually fused with the popular belief in that chimera Progress, were apparent everywhere: in the papers, on the street, in the barber shops: "The fellow who cut my hair—a fine, strapping young fellow, too, nearly six feet high, and with the air of a soldier about him . . . what do you think he discoursed about while he was cutting my hair? The doctrine of evolution, sir, Darwin and Huxley and the lot of them—hashed up somehow with the good time coming and the uni-versal brotherhood, and I don't know what else." [8]

But Darwinism made an equal appeal to the doomsters ever ready to play Cassandra to their age, and in the increasingly skeptical Thomas Henry Huxley they found an authority ready to lend his melancholy note to that swelling symphony of decline: "If for millions of years our globe has taken the upward road, yet sometime the summit will be reached and the downward route be commenced." [9] Such gloomy prognostication was grist for the mills of the Aesthetes, who had from the beginning enjoyed a vested interest in the *fin de siècle* mood, though ironically they turned that mood into more of a myth than it actually was. Despite its stained-glass attitudes and Francesca da Rimini fixations, the Aesthetic movement nursed a central ambiguity in its canon. Pledged to savor with intensity the entire spectrum of human experience, that "appe-

7. Charles Darwin, *The Origin of Species* (New York, 1935), pp. 473–74.
8. Justin McCarthy, *Dear Lady Disdain*, as quoted in Amy Cruse, *The Victorians and Their Reading* (Boston, 1935), p. 97.
9. Thomas Henry Huxley, *Collected Essays* (New York, 1902), IX, 85.

tite for the strange, abnormal and unhealthy," to which George
Moore confessed, and outraging Victorian piety wherever possible,
the Decadents (née Aesthetes) celebrated the aberrant while simultaneously evincing that nostalgia of decay one hears in Dowson's
verse:

> Let us go hence—the night is now at hand;
> The day is overworn, the birds all flown;
> And we have reaped the crops the gods have sown,
> Despair and death; deep darkness over the land,
> Broods like an owl; we cannot understand
> Laughter or tears; for we have only known
> Surpassing vanity: vain things alone
> Have driven our perverse and aimless band.

So both moods, as we know, were present even from the beginning: the strident hopefulness of Vitalists like Wells, Henley, and
Kipling as well as the fashionable *taedium vitae* of Wilde, Dowson,
and Beardsley; and both were in a measure an outgrowth of the
historical cyclicalism that was again coming into vogue toward the
end of the century, a vogue that in turn had taken its lead from that
amazing proliferation of the concept of "developmentalism," an
inevitable outgrowth of Darwinian thought. In the conclusion to
*The Origin of Species* Darwin had appealed for a broader application of his thesis to all the sciences. The wildfire response to that
plea more than exceeded his always modest expectations; and both
the concept and the metaphor of organic evolution became the
unexamined assumption of nineteenth-century science, until finally
it seemed as if "developmentalism" would overwhelm every field of
scientific research, organic and inorganic alike. And Walter Pater
among many others was led to complain that "the idea of development . . . is at last invading one by one, as the secret of their
explanation, all the products of mind. . . . Political constitutions,
again, as we now see so clearly, are 'not made,' cannot be made, but

'grow.' Races, laws, arts, have their origins and end, are themselves ripples only on the great river of organic life. . . ." [10]

The extension of the Darwinian thesis through history and archaeology resulted in that new school of "aesthetic historians," men like the Egyptologist Flinders Petrie, who were busily unearthing among the paintings and shards of the past mute but irrefutable evidence of once-flourishing cultures whose birth, growth, and subsequent decline were clearly discernible in the art and artifacts that had outlived their makers' moment of greatness. Consequently it was only a matter of time before the concern with cultural evolution led to speculation about the contemporary scene, about what stage of development *it* had reached. Men observing the closing years of any century become peculiarly self-conscious about their station in time, the amount of sand left in their hourglass. And as for the late Victorians, used to being thundered at by Carlyle, Arnold, and Ruskin, why, few men of any era had kept a more nervous finger on the pulse of their moral and social well-being. It was a legacy of self-concern the Edwardians were to inherit in barely diminished form; and the organ of that concern was to be essentially the novel, though stripped of Victorian pontification as well as Aesthetic banter. As a character in Wells's *The New Machiavelli* observed, "The day has gone by for either dull responsibility or merely witty art." And between those camps, Impressionists like Ford would pitch their tents, as they strove to make Englishmen aware of those unmistakable signs of cultural deterioration in themselves and their society.

Nowhere was that peculiar Alpha-Omega complex more apparent than in the nation's divided attitude about the moral and psychological implications of the Boer War for the English national temperament. The war was interpreted variously as the final convulsion of a glutted and dying culture and as the ultimate triumph of England's imperial glory. The two-fold reaction to news that Mafeking had

10. Walter Pater, *Plato and Platonism: A Series of Lectures* (London, 1910), pp. 20–21.

been relieved was typical. The *Daily Mail* described the insensate glee with which the London streets greeted the announcement: "London simply went wild with delight. Fleet Street, which, on ordinary nights, contains only its usual number of pedestrians, was, as if by magic, transformed into a thoroughfare crowded and jammed with an excited throng of cheering, shouting, gesticulating, happy people. . . . Women absolutely wept for joy and men threw their arms about each other's necks—strangers' necks for the most part; but that made no difference, for Mafeking was relieved. . . ." [11] Others, like Arnold Bennett and Ford, were appalled by the display of this unsuspected national temper. Bennett, sitting behind the curtains of his study, looked out upon the same scene with less sanguine eyes: "It was distinctly an exhibition of insularity. I must say that I have been quite unable to join with any sincerity in the frantic and hysterical outburst of patriotic enthusiasm of the last few days. Such praise of ourselves as a nation, such gorgeous self-satisfaction and boastfulness are to me painful. . . ." [12]

Such a display was even more painful to Ford, who, with his more acute sense of history, saw the war as a major watershed in the development of the English peoples, an absolute demarcation between past British attitudes and the new days dawning. During their stormy period of collaboration at Aldington, with the interminable squabbles over *le mot juste*, Ford and Conrad did at least agree on the adverse effect the war had upon the "national conscience," as Conrad wrote to Mrs. E. L. Sanderson.[13] But it was Ford who viewed the war as the great turning point in the psychological history of the English peoples: "And then came the Boer War, which appears to me like a chasm separating the new world from the old. Since that period the whole tone of England appears to me to

---

11. *Daily Mail*, May 19, 1900, quoted in Asa Briggs, *They Saw It Happen* (Oxford, 1960), pp. 11–12.
12. *The Journal of Arnold Bennett* (New York, 1932), pp. 106–7.
13. Letter to Mrs. E. L. Sanderson in G. Jean-Aubry, *Joseph Conrad: Life and Letters* (Garden City, N.Y., 1927), I, 294.

have entirely changed. Principles have died out of politics, even as the spirit has died out amongst the practitioners of the arts." [14] In his moments of disgust with the sort of "mawkish flap-doodle" to which Aestheticism had sunk, Ford could speak approvingly of Henley, attributing to him "nearly all that is vital, actual and alive in English work today." [15] And yet he distrusted the rallying cry Henley had chosen to shake England loose from her *fin de siècle* lethargy—that Kiplingesque vision of national destiny that became the stock-in-trade of *The National Observer*, wafted abroad on phrases like "the White Man's Burden" and "the lesser breeds without the law."

Though never so crudely bellicose as the *Daily Mail*, with its self-serving exploitation of British xenophobia, the *Observer's* point of view called out some of the most unsavory aspects of the national psychology: that witless allegiance to Nietzschean arrogance, Nordic jingoism, and the race-glutted pride of the pan-Germanic supremacists. In later years Ford was to recall that during this difficult period "the artistic activities symbolised by the physical force schools of Henley or Mr. Rudyard Kipling were to find, in the world, their counterparts in outrages, wars, rumours of wars, pogroms, repressions." [16] Thus in a literary world that offered only a choice between the art of exhausted nerves and vigorous polemic, Ford, still a young man in his twenties, chose to go his own way, seeking that "isolation from all literary involvements," noted by his recent biographer.[17]

As an Impressionist Ford's ultimate aim was always to play the role of social historian to his age, to present an unbiased account of contemporary moods and tendencies but in the aloof, detached manner of the French Naturalists; commentary and criticism were

14. Ford Madox Ford, *Memories and Impressions* (New York, 1911), p. 171.
15. Ford Madox Ford, *Ancient Lights and Certain New Reflections* (London, 1911), p. 240.
16. Ford Madox Ford, *Return to Yesterday* (New York, 1932), p. 90.
17. Frank MacShane, *The Life and Work of Ford Madox Ford* (New York, 1965), p. 27.

to be implicit in the art itself—not superimposed from without. But in suggesting some viable alternative to contemporary behavior, the novelist must perforce operate from some value system, a difficult task in an age of transition such as the Edwardian when all values were in flux. Such schematization must obviously come from within the artist himself. If he was not the first to recognize it, Ford was one of the first Edwardians to articulate plainly the artist's need to create his own system of values by which he might make some significant commentary on his age. Men might still see life steadily enough; it was becoming increasingly impossible, said Ford, to see it whole: "We have to face [today] such an infinite number of little things that we cannot stay to arrange them in our minds, or to consider them as anything but accidents, happenings, the mere events of the day. And if in outside things we can perceive no design, but only the fortuitous materialism of a bewildering world, we are thrown more and more in upon ourselves for comprehension of that which is not understandable, and for analysis of things of the spirit." [18]

And it was the "spirit," both of England and of the people, that was Ford's most abiding concern. He had analyzed that spirit in a massive work of sociological impressionism entitled *England and the English: An Interpretation*, especially in the third section called "The Spirit of the People." Written between 1904 and 1907, the book is an attempt to "get at the atmosphere" of Ford's own age; and in it he generalizes often and freely about the psychological nature of the English people, particularly about that disconcerting alteration in the modern British mentality. That Ford was consciously creating a conceptual grid by which he could order his own thinking and that it was a purely solipsistic undertaking he makes abundantly clear in the book. After summarizing various attempts to explain the modern temperament he cautioned: "All these things are merely convenient systems of thought by which a man may arrange

18. *Memories and Impressions*, p. 69.

in his mind his mental image of the mundane cosmogony—or they may be systems of thought by which he is able to claim for his particular calling, craft or art, the status of the really important factor in life." [19] Zola had similarly used the empirical method in an effort to elevate the techniques of literature to the dignity of scientific method. With Ford it was an attempt to set up a sweeping tableau of Western history culminating in and explaining the Edwardian period.

Though they are scattered throughout the book, Ford's warnings against taking his historical projections as matters of fact have largely been ignored by critics, who prefer to see them as deeply held convictions. They were not; Ford was too imbued with the historical solipsism of his age to have been guilty of such absolutism. Even of events and characters in the Tudor age, the period of his greatest competence, he was disinclined to dogmatize. After a prolonged study of Henry VIII's private correspondence, Ford came to the conclusion that all speculation where that enigmatic monarch was concerned was apt to go awry: "Should I have found him affable, or terrifying, or seductive, or royal, or courageous? There are so many contradictory facts; there are so many reported interviews, each contradicting the others, so that all I *know* about this king could be reported in the words of Maupassant in introducing one of his characters . . . that he was a gentleman with red whiskers who always went first through a door." [20]

Although Ford was, as I say, one of the earliest novelists to articulate the need for some personal schematization of reality during a period of cultural breakdown, the late-Victorian period had already witnessed art's instinctive response to the problem in the approach of writers like Wells, Davidson, and Butler. They represent the Alpha wing of those writers who found in the notion of

19. Ford Madox Ford, *England and the English: An Interpretation* (New York, 1907), p. 277.
20. Ford Madox Ford, "On Impressionism I," *Poetry and Drama*, II, 2 (June, 1914), p. 171.

process positive hope for improvement of the human condition, ruthless of individual fate though that process might be. Ford, as we shall see, belongs to the nay-sayers of the Omega wing who saw in historical process that gradual deterioration of Western culture. But in both instances the assumption of some sort of evolutionary process lies behind the two moods, for the theory of evolution itself, when applied to society, may have either positive or negative connotations. In itself, it is a perfectly neutral conception, lending itself equally to theories of decline or improvement, of death or rebirth. Why a man should opt for the one rather than the other is a matter of education, background, and temperament—as it was with Ford.

H. G. Wells, for example, found the answer both to his fear of personal extinction and to Edwardian political anarchy in that shaky fusion of Schopenhauer and Darwin. Here the individual life becomes merely a passing phase of the "greater life," an individual component of inexorable "process." Individual will and purpose are swallowed up within that larger being, as all self-concern is left behind. Naturally those who best serve this shadowy "larger being" will prosper; those who do not must, unfortunately, be weeded out. Wells's positive reading of Darwin and his affirmative reaction to the concept of process led him perilously close to the Nietzschean arrogance of his less enlightened brethren, who were less aware than he of the danger. Consequently he has one traditionalist reply contemptuously to his hero Remington's scheme for an aristocracy of culture: "Superman rubbish—Nietzsche!" Gradually Wells turned more fully from Schopenhauer to Darwin, believing the latter had explained more convincingly the process Schopenhauer had only intuited; but in both cases the motivation had been the same—an escape from the relativistic chaos and political anarchy of the day into some purposeful pattern of historical evolution. It was to become an increasingly common intellectual and artistic response over the next decade.

Another Alpha voice raised amidst the prophets of doom, and which likewise founded its optimism on progressive evolution, was that of John Davidson (1857–1909). Among its lesser figures, the nineties produced no mind more remarkable than that of this poet-philosopher. The skeptical son of a Scottish evangelical minister, Davidson turned early to science—that same science that had unsettled the old dispensations—as a possible foundation for a new philosophy of purposeful existence; but, as so often happens, the philosopher destroyed what there was of the native artist in him. After a few desultory years of private- and public-school teaching, and lured by the possibility of a literary career, he arrived in London in 1899. Though he was an early contributor to the *Yellow Book* and a member of the Rhymer's Club, he constantly parodied Aesthetic pretensions and postures in works like *Baptist Lake* (1894) and *Earl Lavender* (1895); and from 1891 to 1899 published his two collections of *Fleet Street Eclogues*, as well as a number of ballad series. Increasingly unable to capture or hold any sympathetic audience and progressively disillusioned by his own failure to discover any positive creed, he became increasingly alienated from that late Victorian society he once described as literally "flowering with suns and systems."

Davidson's despair was to generate one of those peculiarly personal and eclectic "systems" that became increasingly common among artists during these years. In a remarkable series of *Testaments*—an attempt to synthesize the thought of Nietzsche, Wagner, Darwin, and Carlyle—Davidson invoked the authority of evolutionary doctrine to defend British overseas policy, as well as that developing mood of intransigency, as a part of ineluctable "process." Influenced by Nietzsche's concept of the *Übermensch*—in his mind the ultimate and achieved end of evolution—Davidson gave unhesitating support to the doctrines of the racial supremacists, embodied in the figure of the modern Englishman, a figure he celebrated in both prose and verse: "The Englishman is the Overman: and the history of England is the history of his evolution." [21] Discussing the

21. John Davidson, *The Testament of John Davidson* (London, 1908), p. 18.

the humanist's need for
y he himself referred to as
ashioned his later fiction,
*rewhon Revisited*, although
of his later qualification of

fter the appearance of *The*
y example of the evolutionary
f men cut off from the outside
es, embody those peculiar varia-
m. Convinced by one of their
eril of being replaced by his own
e destroyed all but their simplest
neo-Darwinian society, which has
skin and Morris, reflects the same
were to be the core of Davidson's
consciousness from fire, to rock, to
an. Only man, now aware that he may
bsolete by the next stage, the machine
rt the evolutionary process by denying
ems logically to aim at the machine as the

m is affirmed but modified; and "prog-
, can have unfortunate consequences. It is
Wisdom at the College of Unreason who
from the outer world why Erewhon has
rogress: "I [the visitor] ventured feebly to
how progress could be made in any art or
anything at all, without more or less self-seek-
ability. 'Of course it cannot,' said the Professor,
bject to progress.'" Though but a part of the
book, the professor's argument has a trenchancy
zed, and that seemed to Ford and Conrad the evil
lling the whole concept of Progress. It is the

reigning psychological mood in Edwardian England, Ford had arrived at very nearly the same conclusion in the third section of
*England and the English*, though for him it seemed tragedy rather
than triumph, for the Overman mentality seemed an absolute abro-
gation of the traditional English national psychology, a thesis he
would attempt to dramatize in *The Inheritors*. He could not, like
Davidson, take comfort in the thought that such a temperament, as
well as the international quarrels it occasioned, was a logical and
defensible extension of the struggle for existence between superior
and inferior species—that "new unhallowed song" to which Davidson, among others, was urging Englishmen to tune their pipes:

> We recognize at last
>     That war is not of God.
> Wherefore we now uplift
>     Our new unhallowed song:
> The race is to the swift,
>     The battle to the strong.[22]

Consequently, by one of those paradoxical twists of intellectual
history, the optimism generated by the writing and lecturing of
Darwin, Huxley, Tyndall, and Spencer concerning the future of
mankind led quite directly to that concept of the Nietzschean
demi-god—pitiless and unscrupulous—who would lead England out
of the "slackness, mental dishonesty, presumption, mercenary respectability and sentimentalized commercialism of the Victorian
period," as Wells had prophesied in *The New Machiavelli*. Both he
and Davidson were spokesmen for that frame of mind permeating
their society from top to bottom, from the xenophobia of the man in
the street, with his glib assurance of the benefits of Progress, to Lord
Rosebery's championship of "efficiency" above all before the as-
sembled House of Lords. A few like Ford and Conrad saw the dark
side of the vision as well, which the latter once described in this way:

22. John Davidson, "War Song," *Selected Poems* (London, 1905).

"Progress leaves its dead by the way, for progress is onl~
adventure as its leaders and chiefs know very well in ·'
is a march into an undiscovered country; and ir
the victims do not count." [23] And from these "
counted and uncountable, Ford was to create hi.
protagonists.

That there would always be those who counted t.
than the gain was equally clear to Ford's friend Master.
member of Asquith's cabinet and a social analyst to v
Ford and Conrad owe more than has been recognized.
[Masterman wrote] discern a body raising always a banner
defiance of the newer changes in moral law, and gathering ar
as a centre all the re-actions from the hurried progress of thing
picturesque rallies towards the worship of an older time, al.
whom the lethargy of the decent and the ignobly decent, and t.
severe technical outlook of a scientific world, are remote anc
hostile." [24] It was just such a banner that Ford and Conrad were to
raise in *The Inheritors*, with its allegorical attack upon the new
Nietzschean dynamic. The novel darkly, though artlessly, implied
that the Wellsian credo of New Republicanism was but another
form of that deterioration of traditional English values. As we will
see later, Ford and Conrad were self-consciously pressing the Nietzschean assumption to its ultimate and ruthless conclusion.

What is interesting in Davidson for this study is the fact that his
artistic response to the late Victorian shambles is so peculiarly
parallel to Ford's. Both draw upon that general mood of despair as
well as the specific teachings—pure or diluted—of Darwin,
Nietzsche, and Schopenhauer; but where the ideas of these men held
a promise of hope for temperaments like Davidson and Wells, they
boded only ill to the minds of others, like Ford and Conrad. Davidson, whom Ford once met briefly at the home of Ernest Rhys, was

23. Joseph Conrad, "The Crime of Partition" in *Notes on Life and Letters*
(London, 1925), p. 118.
24. C. F. G. Masterman, *In Peril of Change* (New York, n.d.), p. 320.

subsequent dehumanization of man, brought about by an increasingly technocratic society, that Ford and Conrad were allegorizing in *The Inheritors*. Published in the same year (1901) as the enlarged version of *Erewhon*, *The Inheritors* really belongs to that dying genre, the evolutionary romance—a fact so far unrecognized by critics.

In *The Inheritors* the world, beginning with England, is about to be taken over by a cold, calculating species new on the world scene. Although the satiric intent of the book was perfectly evident, almost to the point of libel, the trappings of allegorical fantasy made the novel the least characteristic that either Ford or Conrad ever wrote. The reason was obvious enough; both were working in a genre uncongenial to their genius and one already in a state of decline. The tradition of the genre stretches from even earlier than Bulwer-Lytton's *The Coming Race* (1871), a novel similar in many respects to *Erewhon*, down to Henry Curwen's *Zit and Xoe*, published in the closing year of the nineteenth century. All made much use of popularized notions of evolution, often simply exploiting the more sensational aspects of Darwinism. But for the more serious novelist, it created a new dimension in the satiric novel.

Only partially characteristic of the evolutionary romance, *Zit and Xoe* shows graphically the deep and pervasive influence of Darwin. Between them Zit and Xoe, two specimens of prehistoric man, telescope man's entire evolutionary development within their single lifetimes. But recently descended from the trees, they quickly discover the use of tools, go on to master agronomy and navigation, and settle down in ripe old age to the achievement of a written language. Unlike the author of *Zit and Xoe*, H. G. Wells in *A Story of the Stone Age* chose to focus on one moment in the evolutionary drama, the discovery of the flint-headed axe, which made paleolithic man the fittest to survive. And Thomas Hardy, avoiding the literal approach of *Zit and Xoe*, unrolls the pageant of human development in a single moment of vision as the geologist-hero of *A Pair of Blue Eyes* dangles from a cliff face, staring at a prehistoric fossil:

Time closed up like a fan before him. He saw himself at one extremity of the years, face to face with the beginning and all the intermediate centuries simultaneously. Fierce men, clothed in hides of beasts, and carrying, for defense and attack, huge clubs and pointed spears, rose from the rock, like the phantoms before the doomed Macbeth. . . . Behind them stood an earlier band. No man was there. Huge elephantine forms, the mastodon . . . the megatherium, and the myledon—all, for the moment, in juxtaposition.[30]

But in exploiting the satiric possibilities of evolutionary thought, the novelist's most common recourse was to those forgotten lands where man, or some man-like creature, had evolved along a different evolutionary path. Sometimes the society is exemplary, and satiric effect depends on audience recognition of its own inadequacy by contrast with these superior beings. At other times the suggestion is of a coming race of cold rationalists, whose reign augurs ill for the future of mankind. In Robert Dudgeon's *Colymbia* (1873), the hero is shipwrecked on an isolated island of aqua-men, not unlike the dispassionate inhabitants of Houyhnhnmland. In W. H. Hudson's *A Crystal Age* (1887), a young man blunders into an advanced civilization where man has evolved beyond the storm and stress of human passions, and where he finally succumbs—unable to make the transition to their advanced temperament.

Repeatedly in novels like Malet's *Colonel Enderby's Wife* (1885) or H. B. Marriott Watson's *Marahuna* (1896), evolutionary doctrine is invoked to explain the emergence of a human temperament antithetical to traditional Western idealism. Because of its ruthless dismissal of outmoded concepts like altruism and honor, the new temperament always has an advantage over older, more compassionate human types. Discussing the literature of regressive evolution, Leo Henkin concludes that in these novels "man's life on earth is represented largely as a battle in which the beautiful and humane natures are driven to the wall by the small-minded, the mercenary, the rapacious, or the ruthlessly efficient."[31] Such was Ford's own

30. Thomas Hardy, *A Pair of Blue Eyes* (New York, n.d.), p. 253.
31. Leo Henkin, *Darwinism in the English Novel: 1860–1910* (New York, 1963), p. 223.

analysis of the human situation, and it is the fate he metes out to all of his major protagonists, who are hunted down and destroyed by that same process of environmental determinism Dowell describes near the close of *The Good Soldier:* "Conventions and traditions, I suppose, work blindly but surely for the preservation of the normal type; for the extinction of proud, resolute, and unusual individuals. . . . So Edward and Nancy found themselves steamrolled out and Leonora survives, the perfectly normal type, married to a man who is rather like a rabbit. . . . So those splendid and tumultuous creatures with their magnetism and their passions . . . have gone from this earth." [32]

So it is with all of Ford's splendid and tumultuous protagonists who are inevitably ground down by the workings of a private evolutionary mythos Ford created in an attempt to analyze, and later dramatize, the cultural collapse he discerned around him. It was through his theory of an evolving national will that Ford sought to explain, by a continuing contrast of past and present, the decay of traditional English values. In an age that has lost its sense of values the artist's problem is to locate some affirmative and sympathetic response for behavioral patterns now generally felt to be outmoded. With eclecticism and moral relativism corroding all fixed standards of judgment, a novelist like Ford could no longer count upon his reader's outrage at seeing old-fashioned idealists outmaneuvered by political realists and pragmatists. A fading Christian ethos might still opt for the former, but its authority was seriously challenged by social Darwinists who pointed to those "natural" laws of survival, supposedly operative in both jungle and society, which gave sanction to efficiency and success before all else. As a character in a novel of the eighties had bitterly put it: "Ah! what an inspiring and consolatory doctrine is that of the survival of the fittest. How agreeably it strengthens the hands of the capable, merciless strong, and causes the gentle and timid weak to duck under. How beauti-

32. Ford Madox Ford, *The Good Soldier*, in *The Bodley Head Ford Madox Ford*, ed. Graham Greene (London, 1962), p. 205. (All subsequent references will be to this edition.)

fully it is calculated to increase the exercise of the more robust virtues—pride, arrogance, cruelty, and such like." [33]

Satiric though the passage is, it points the way toward that growing problem in the breakdown of shared values between novelist and reader. If Nature herself sanctions the ultimate success of the strong and efficient, how can the artist ask his audience—increasingly apt to accept the scientist's word—to admire or sympathize with the "gentle and timid weak," those obviously unfitted to function or even survive in modern society? This becomes, in large measure, the problem with all Ford's major protagonists. Why should they seem exemplary when they are so obviously wrongheaded and out of touch with their times? And this is as true of the historical figures as it is of the modern. Katherine Howard in the sixteenth century, Edward Colman in the seventeenth, as well as Edward Ashburnham and Christopher Tietjens in the twentieth—all are equally vestigial for the historical periods they find themselves born into. Throughout the early novels—from *The Inheritors* to *The Good Soldier*—Ford was to rely increasingly upon a behind-the-scenes theory of psychological and historical evolution that largely predetermines the fate of these protagonists.

Hardly less spectacular than many of its predecessors in the evolutionary romance, *The Inheritors* reflects Ford's own regressive view of Darwinian evolution. In it the Englishman, with his traditional ideals of honor and altruism, is about to be displaced by a new, vigorous, but totally unscrupulous type. Years later in *Joseph Conrad: A Personal Remembrance*, Ford was to recall his and Conrad's first collaboration as "a political work, rather allegorically backing Mr. Balfour in the then government; the villain was to be Joseph Chamberlain who had made the war." [34] The "war" of course was the Boer War, which, through its mood of pitiless arrogance, had first alerted Ford to the possibility that traditional

---

33. Lucas Malet, *Colonel Enderby's Wife* (London, 1911), II, 85.
34. Ford Madox Ford, *Joseph Conrad: A Personal Remembrance* (New York, 1965), p. 141.

English attitudes and values might be changing, what he was later to describe as "a change in the national psychology." [35] The novel was to depict allegorically the newly emergent forces of unprincipled opportunism in English politics.

The protagonist, a young journalist named Etchingham Granger, finds himself poised—like so many of Ford's later protagonists—between two worlds, the old and the new. The past with its burden of political responsibility and integrity is represented by Granger's friend, the foreign minister Churchill. Challenging the old order for which he stands is a group of shadowy, semimysterious figures out of the fourth dimension. These "dimensionists," physically indistinguishable from their human counterparts, are described to Granger by one of their number, a young woman to whose will he eventually succumbs: "a race clear-sighted, eminently practical, incredible; with no ideals, prejudices or remorse; with no feeling for art and no reverence for life; free from any ethical tradition; callous to pain, weakness, suffering and death. . . ." [36]

Granger, the member of a class whose moral fibre has eroded through Victorian materialism and glut, watches in dumb fascination as the unscrupulous dimensionists discredit Churchill, his party, and the entire tradition of nineteenth-century liberal humanism. Historically, however, the dimensionists go beyond being a mere satiric embodiment of Chamberlainism, the New Hedonism, the New Republicanism, *Daily Mail* xenophobia, or what have you. They represent a calling out of all those forces of illiterate racism, imperialistic arrogance, and national parochialism that found their *raison d'être* in Darwin, who as Ford once wrote, "has done more to change the psychology of the western world than any man since Jean Jacques Rousseau. . . ." [37] And it was this changing English psychology that Ford was to chronicle in all his major novels

35. *England and the English*, p. 354.
36. Ford Madox Ford and Joseph Conrad, *The Inheritors: An Extravagant Story* (New York, 1924), p. 120.
37. Ford Madox Ford, *The Critical Attitude* (London, 1911), p. 117.

between 1901 and 1915; and always caught in the middle was Ford's man of honor—quaint, vestigial, and doomed.

The Inheritors is as much a reply to Wells's New Republicanism as it is to the Davidsonian hero and that whole sorry rout of social reformers, unfettered by any moral or ethical tradition, who go crashing through the social jungle, establishing with unblinking ruthlessness a new order built on the ruins of an outdated democratic humanism, and ruled over by the Nietzschean Overman similar to Ostrog in Wells's When the Sleeper Wakes. Though Wells publicly denounced an imperialism that justified itself in Darwinian doctrine, his increasingly Benthamite distrust of all traditional guideposts in seeking a way out of the Edwardian impasse never failed to irritate Ford's ingrained Tory paternalism with its deep distrust of all "Übermensch" schemes for social regeneration.

That Ford and Conrad were aware of the Nietzschean implications of The Inheritors is clear from a letter Conrad wrote to Ford describing his interview with their publisher, who was understandably nervous over the possibility of libel proceedings. Conrad had hastened to assure him, half facetiously, that the attitudes of mind fictionalized in the novel were inevitably "what Nietzsche's philosophy leads to . . . your overman," and that far from libeling contemporary political figures what they had done was to "attack not individuals, but the spirit of the age." [38] Although the female dimensionist bears some slight resemblance to that new figure beginning to appear in the novels of the nineties, the amoral heroine, Ford and Conrad saw her as the embodiment of that pro-Boer War temperament, vaguely termed Nietzschean, increasingly eulogized by pseudo-ethnologists like Houston Chamberlain and Grant Allen. In slightly modulated tones the same note was being sounded by Henley, Wells, and Kipling who sometimes confused it with their own brand of Heroic Vitalism.

38. Letter from Joseph Conrad to Ford Madox Ford (1903) in G. Jean-Aubry, Joseph Conrad: Life and Letters (New York, 1927), I, 313.

Though in later years Ford dismissed *The Inheritors* as hack work
—despite Conrad's insistence that it was "a damn good book"—the
novel constitutes a crucial phase in Ford's development as a social
historian. Throughout the novel there are suggestions of a larger
natural process at work, a process that explains in crude evolutionary terms the mechanics of the psychological changes now taking
place in England. In a narrative closely reminiscent of Bulwer-Lytton's *The Coming Race*, the female dimensionist explains to the
earthling Granger the initial sundering of their once-common species at some point in prehistory into two divergent streams, streams
entailing that typical pattern of birth, growth, and decay: "Your
ancestors were [also] mine, but long ago you were crowded out of
the Dimension as we are to-day, you overran the earth as we shall
tomorrow. But you contracted diseases, as we shall contract them,
—beliefs, traditions; fears; ideas of pity. . . . of love. You grow
luxurious in the worship of your ideals . . . ; you solaced yourselves
with creeds, with arts—you have forgotten." [39] What mankind has
"forgotten," under the moderating influence of civilization, is the
elemental nature of human strife, "a really very relentless warfare"
as Conrad once described it in *Notes on Life and Letters*,[40] and later
dramatized in his portrait of London as a primeval swamp in *The
Secret Agent*. And those ironic "diseases" from which western man
suffers—"beliefs," "traditions" and "pity"—are those that symbolically afflict all of Ford's major protagonists.

Speculation over the possibility of an individual or a group being
cut off from the main line of evolution and thereby developing
along a different path, with subsequent temperamental variations,
was one of the stock devices of the evolutionary romance. It became
a major satiric technique in depicting the cruel and unnatural in
human behavior in novels like Bulwer-Lytton's *The Coming Race*,
Watson's *Marahuna*, Hudson's *A Crystal Age*, as well as Rider

39. Ford and Conrad, *The Inheritors*, p. 10.
40. *Notes on Life and Letters*, p. 18.

Haggard's *She* and dozens of others. The most "scientific" of all these fabulists, H. G. Wells, once noted his own use of this device for his *Time Machine* (1894): "The future depicted in the *Time Machine* was a mere fantasy based on the idea of the human species developing about divergent lines. . . ." [41] But neither a pseudoscientific topicality nor narrative sensationalism sufficed to save the evolutionary romance from the same extinction it had meted out to its subjects. The genre has faded from literary memory even as Ford and Conrad's earliest collaboration has nearly done—and rightly so.

More than any of Ford's later novels, those based on a more tenable theory of psychological and temperamental evolution, *The Inheritors* comes dangerously close to the *roman à thèse*. The novel was crippled from the outset, not only by its burden of realistic social concern—so at odds with its metaphysical trapping—but by a flatness of characterization it shares in common with most of these romances. Such flattening can be but partially justified by the authors' stated intention of dealing "not with individuals, but the spirit of the age." The statement itself represents that Zolaesque heritage under which influence both men worked, that subordination of character to social diagnostics that Wells, in a review of Gissing, described as "displaying a group of typical individuals at the point of action of some great social force, the social force in question and not the 'hero' or 'heroine' being the real operative interest of the story." [42]

Ford realized later that in seeking to escape from the social unconcern of the Aesthetic movement as well as the obtrusive moralizing of the Victorians, the Impressionist faced a formidable problem in balancing social diagnostics with the felt life of the novel, without the novelist meanwhile showing his face. Ford's artistic failure at this point in his career is reminiscent of Davidson's.

41. *Experiment in Autobiography*, p. 550.
42. H. G. Wells, "The Novels of Mr. George Gissing," *Contemporary Review*, LXII (August, 1897), 193.

Though writers like Davidson and Butler had pointed a way out of the impasse created by the breakdown of standards of values, once linking artist and audience, Davidson at least was fated never to reach that audience, and Butler but briefly and after his death. The personal cosmogony each had sought to create on a scientific foundation of Darwinism and "process" was too intensely subjective in its reading of social evolution, and the philosopher too often overshadowed the artist; the popular imagination was not caught. With Ford it was to be different, but not until after a period of experimentation.

The failure of *The Inheritors* behind him, Ford sought over the next decade for some means by which to suggest *implicitly* the contrast between traditional English values and the new national temper he saw emerging from the Boer War. The possibility of some artistically definable process of social selectivity abroad in the world continued to appeal to him, though ultimately he was to search elsewhere—through English history—for the means of rendering that evolutionary process dramatically convincing in his novels. Although *The Inheritors* anticipates Ford's lifelong concern with the contemporary scene, the novel fails to dramatize convincingly the scope and workings of that historical process of growth and decay which lay behind the cultural collapse of Edwardian society, as Ford visualized it to himself. The Fourth Dimension had not proved a convincing counter against which to weigh England's venerable past. Only after retreating in time from the contemporary scene to the historical past of the Katherine Howard trilogy, did Ford discover a technique by which to dramatize that deterministic law of historical survival and extinction which broods over all his major works.

# 2. The Four Ages of Man

Ford criticism to date has erred in seeking to isolate just this or that attribute of the Fordian hero (usually a vague Christian altruism), and then proceeding to a cross-indexing of all the protagonists, showing how each measures up to or falls short of the mean. The fundamental error has been to overlook the fact that it is not the temperaments of these protagonists that is similar but rather the type of struggle in which each is embroiled. Their conflict stems from a struggle against an uncongenial "Time Spirit," as both Ford and Hegel phrased it, which gives short shrift to their personal codes of honor or behavior. In themselves these protagonists are as different from one another as human beings inevitably are—except when we simplify them for the sake of specious generalization. Probably the compelling force behind these attempts to categorize Ford's hero has been that conditioned critical tendency to place Ford in the late-Victorian tradition of liberal humanism that sought to recover the "essence" of Christianity from the char and rubble of the fundamentalist ruin. Although many of Ford's typical innocents, with their loosely Christian virtues, find themselves standing high and dry on

Arnold's Dover Beach, Ford himself had few illusions about the fate contemporary society would mete out to these vestigial survivors of an older ethical tradition. His pessimism generated a deterministic theory of historical movement that explains quite clearly the common bond between Ford's protagonists by establishing a single pattern of dramatic conflict for reach.

A potpourri of late-nineteenth-century historical theory, Ford's outline of English history combines the movement of Hegelianism with the mechanics of "Darwinian" social selection, while the whole is saturated with that late *fin de siècle* gloom that had gradually attached itself, in the minds of many, to those notions of process and historical change. From the eighteen-twenties down to mid-century, German intellectual thought had been largely dominated by Hegelian idealism, with its surface optimism about the direction of human history. As Hegel himself had phrased it: "Universal history . . . shows the development of the consciousness of Freedom on the part of the Spirit, and of the consequent realizations of that Freedom." [1] In realizing that "Freedom" Hegel argued that history moved through successive cycles or "gradations" of conflict and resolution, always tending towards social improvement. If the rash of social reforms in England during the thirties and forties seemed to augur well, the bitter opposition to their passage served as a constant reminder that forces antithetical to progress always existed—if only to be overcome.

Social awareness of such class struggle, solemnized by Marx, was imprinted on the popular mind by the "two nations" theme of Disraeli and Dickens. But by mid-century Hegelianism was already in retreat and, along with it, its explanation of historical movement. The new idol of the intellectual market place, Darwinism, with that tremendous proliferation of the idea of "process," insinuated itself into every area of intellectual speculation. It was only a matter of

1. Georg Wilhelm Friedrich Hegel, *The Philosophy of History*, trans. J. Sibree (New York, 1956), p. 63.

time before Darwinian gradualism replaced the "catastrophic" notions of Hegel. It was evolution and not revolution that was now seen to be the real movement of history—a slow organic alteration of all things in time, with a past eternally present but never repeating itself in exactly fixed cycles but rather by successive modulations, evolving ever new variations. The eighteenth-century mechanistic assumptions of Hegel had given way before the new organic metaphor of Darwinian process. Unfortunately Hegelian *idealism* was also forced to retreat before those ancillary Darwinian implications—the evolutionary process could not guarantee the sort of qualitative improvement implicit in Hegelian idealism. And as the century wore on and the Victorian dream faded, the possibility of regressive evolution, in terms of both society and the individual, became alarmingly apparent. As such it was but another aspect of that collective sense of decline and decay that is one of the hallmarks of the late Victorian and Edwardian intellectual climate.

It was Ford's attempt "to get at the spirit" of this age that led him back over England's historic past, seeking out some pattern in the development of the English national spirit. Although there are both implicit and explicit references to his system scattered throughout Ford's work from *Hans Holbein* (1905) to *Great Trade Route* (1937), Ford first alluded to it most fully in *The Spirit of the People*, published later as the third section of *England and the English: An Interpretation* (1907). As we shall see later, the pattern had already begun to emerge in Ford's fiction as early as 1906 in *The Fifth Queen* and in his nonfiction as early as the Holbein monograph published a year earlier. But the fullest explication appears in *England and the English*. An admittedly personal and impressionistic reading of England's past, the theory supposes a gradual psychological evolution of the British people from the middle ages down to the moment of writing. At one point, broadening the scope of his theory to include the whole of Western culture, Ford argued "that the psychology of the civilized world changes—that the dominant types of the world alter with changing, if mysterious, alterations in the economic or social conditions of the races."[2] The "dominant types" Ford postulates are those individuals in every generation who best sum up in their ideals and actions the moods and assumptions of their respective societies. Such an individual becomes the embodiment of the national will in a given historical setting.

Ford's theory of dominant psychological types, of outstanding historical personages, not always those remembered in history books, was by no means original with him. It was a staple of the Hegelian legacy itself and had taken its place as unexamined assumption with a subsequent generation of historians, both professional and amateur. Ford had simply pressed these types into service as the crucial personae of his "mundane cosmogony." Hegel had described these dominant types as "World Historical Individuals," men whose thought, action, and character reflect the larger spirit of the times. And Taine as well had argued in his *History of English Literature* that English history had witnessed a continual alteration of its "national genius," its successive dominant temperaments: "A certain dominant idea has had sway; men . . . have taken to themselves a certain ideal model of man. . . . This creative and universal idea is displayed over the whole field of action and thought; and after covering the world with its involuntarily systematic works, it has faded, it has died away, and lo, a new idea springs up, destined to a like domination. . . ."[3] There is no evidence, either positive or negative, to suggest Ford's familiarity with Taine, although there is hardly an idea, assertion, or assumption in Ford's comments upon English race, culture, or history that cannot be found in Taine, which is only to suggest their extreme currency. It is impossible to prove any direct influence of Hegel or Taine upon Ford, who may or may not have read them. What is known is that Hegel had a profound influence upon at least one school of British historians

2. Ford Madox Ford, *England and the English: An Interpretation* (New York, 1907), p. 277.
3. Hippolyte A. Taine, *History of English Literature*, trans. H. Van Laun (New York, 1965), I, 22–23.

during the eighteen-sixties and -seventies—the so-called Oxford school. And it was the most successful and widely acclaimed scholar of this school from whom Ford drew most of his ideas about English history, as we shall see later.

The Darwinian and Hegelian overtones of Ford's system become apparent as he explains the relation of his successive dominant types to power struggles both within and between national states: "The nation that will best survive the struggle for existence is the nation that shall contain the largest number of individuals . . . fitted to deal with the peculiar circumstances of that age. . . ." [4] That is, whatever type of man and ability the age requires for pre-eminence, the nation that produces the largest proportion of such types will inevitably dominate the others. If it is a military age, the nation that produces the militarist will come to the fore. And the same procedure follows for ages of discovery, expansion, settlement, or commerce. For all his larger idealism, even Hegel was forced to admit that where individual worth was concerned there were serious drawbacks to the progress of the "World Spirit" as it moved towards self-realization: "They who on moral grounds, and consequently with noble intention, have resisted that which the advance of the World Spirit makes necessary, stand higher in moral worth than those whose crimes have been turned into the means—under the direction of a superior principle—of realizing that principle." [5] Thus Katherine Howard in *The Fifth Queen* may stand "higher in moral worth" than Thomas Cromwell—singled out by Ford as the dominant type of the Tudor age—but she will be as inexorably "steam-rolled out" as are Nancy Rufford and Edward Ashburnham in *The Good Soldier*, all victims of the same historical process that Ford made the backbone of his novels between 1901 and 1915. It was a concern Ford shared in common with his contemporaries in the novel, what I. A. Richards once referred to, in connection with

---

4. *England and the English*, pp. 277–88.
5. *The Philosophy of History*, p. 67.

Forster, as "almost an obsession with the preservation of certain strains and the disappearance of others. . . ."

Ford's approach to history was understandably not that of academe, nor or those "veracity-mad" researchers whose "mole-work lucubrations" he loudly and consistently condemned.[6] Yet despite the imaginative sweep of his historical imagination as it rolled over entire centuries, Ford never confused the roles of Clio and Calliope. Their sister realms, History and Art, though related, were hardly interchangeable, although by the end of the nineteenth century, with the growth of solipsistic history, historians themselves had begun to blur the distinctions, admitting the imagination to an ever greater role in the reconstruction of the past. History, taking its lead from the sciences, had sought to ground its techniques upon the so-called law of "cause and effect," realizing only belatedly that such laws were inapplicable to the study of human affairs. What facts of history are available, argued men like Trevelyan, do not lend themselves to mechanistic analysis. Sensible to the achievement of Pollard in imaginatively reconstructing Tudor England—a book that spiked Ford's own historical ambitions—Trevelyan argued that the genuine historian must have more than an aggregate knowledge of facts: "To give a true picture of any country, or man or group of men, in the past requires industry and knowledge, for only the documents can tell us the truth, but it requires also insight, sympathy and imagination of the finest, and, last but not least, the art of making our ancestors live again in modern narrative." [7]

Ford the artist, faced with much the same problem as the historians, sought to impose on England's past and present a pattern of growth and decay, his "private and particular image." On such would he ground an art dedicated to analyzing the contemporary moment as the end result of the long "process" of history. In Ford's mind that process resolved itself into four successive and distinctive

6. For a perfectly characteristic statement, see Ford's "Dedication" to *A Little Less than Gods* (New York, 1928).

7. G. M. Trevelyan, *Clio, A Muse and Other Essays* (London, 1913), p. 151.

periods, beginning with the middle ages or, more specifically, the period of feudal England. It was inevitable that Ford should have been drawn to this period as a starting point, not simply because its waning years suggested the same flux and uncertainty as the Edwardian age but because the Pre-Raphaelite surroundings of his youth had accustomed him to the sights, the sentiments, and the trappings of feudalism. Through these and his early readings in history it was the landscape he knew best, and its imagined scenes, to the end of his life, always beckoned as his own "Happy Isles."

Beginning with the feudal period, Ford divides British history into four great psychological ages, each exemplifying a specific dominant personality type with distinguishing social, economic, and religious assumptions that sum up the general temper or "spirit" of the people for that particular age. The first of Ford's four ages of man is the "pre-Tudor" age, dating from late Anglo-Saxondom down to the Battle of Bosworth in 1485. The years between 1485 and the 1530s represent a troublous period of transition between feudalism and the England of the New Learning—a period of conflict, both physical and theoretical, in the religious, political, and economic life of the nation. The second period is the "Tudor-Stuart" age, which reaches down to the Glorious Revolution of 1688 and the installation of William of Orange. This period, like the one preceding it, goes through progressive cycles of birth, growth, and decay, finally giving way to the third period, which Ford designates as the "modern age," covering approximately the eighteenth and nineteenth centuries. It is this historical period, along with its ethical assumptions and dominant psychological type, that Ford sensed was coming to a close during the Edwardian era. Even as he wrote, under the shadow of the Boer War, Ford was dimly aware of some new shift in the psychological temper of the English people that was bringing a totally different dominant type to the fore with a relentless repudiation of old standards of belief and conduct, a restless impatience with the outworn values of a Tietjens or Ashburnham. The traditions for which Tietjens and Ashburnham stood, Ford felt, were now drawing to a close: "We imagine perhaps a change in the national psychology. And I am quite prepared to have it said that these pages—if they get at any spirit at all—get only at a national spirit that is already on the wane." [8]

What might be the dominant characteristics of this fourth age, what its new dominant type, Ford was not fully prepared to say, but he does suggest its general nature in all of his novels set in the contemporary scene—a world devoid of honor, principles, and faith; derelict in its sense of moral obligation; irresponsibly deaf to the old verities and ruthless in its destruction of those who remembered—men like George Moffat, Don Kelleg, Edward Ashburnham, and Christopher Tietjens. How had this come about? Ford traced the slow, inexorable evolution of the nation's psychological development from medievalism onwards.

Ford's imaginative reconstruction of medieval England was a more forthright and less ingenuous account than that of the Pre-Raphaelites and also a flat rejection of William Morris, who, as Ford wrote, "had never looked medievalism, with its cruelties, its filth, its stenches, and its avarice, in the face. . . ." [9] Such an age, Ford went on, inevitably brought to the fore a dominant psychological type best equipped to survive in a rough, out-of-doors existence, one capable of unreflecting violence in the pursuit of social and political ends: ". . . upon the whole, speaking impressionistically—we may say that the mediaeval history of Western Europe before the fifteenth century, and the history of England in particular during that period, leaves upon the mind the impression of being a matter, or a long series of matters, decided by sword blows. Before, as a rule, the king was a man who smashed his opponent over the head with a heavy mace and set upon his brows the circlet that he found hanging to a thorn bush." [10]

Although the image obviously suggests Henry VII at Bosworth

8. *England and the English*, p. 354.
9. Ford Madox Ford, *Memories and Impressions* (New York, 1911), p. 18.
10. *England and the English*, p. 280.

Field, Ford felt this particular type was best exemplified in men like the Black Prince, Du Guesclin or Joan of Arc in France, or the old Earl of Norfolk during the reign of Henry VIII. Though Ford was, as he said, "speaking impressionistically," he was also echoing a popular and commonplace image long associated with the heyday of feudalism, one still current in his own time. Hegel earlier had, to be sure, pointed to the "martial spirit" of feudalism as its most significant feature.[11] And though Taine reiterated Hegel's observations, noting the "habits of violent activity . . . the savagery, ignorance, and passions of feudal life,"[12] the whole concept had been given renewed emphasis by popular ethnologists like Houston Stewart Chamberlain, zealous in their championship of the Wagnerite ideal, the Germanic medieval spirit. Chamberlain, the most enthusiastic and voluble of the pan-Germanists, describes the medieval type even as Ford had envisioned him: "this type in England . . . on horseback, swinging his battle-axe to protect his beloved northern home. . . ."[13] Ford, as we shall see later, borrowed heavily from the theories and speculations of current ethnology.

In Ford's mind such individuals were both type and symbol of an age where violence and brutality were ready token in every leafy byway and palace corridor, where reflection and diplomacy played no part in the winning and retaining of crown or mitre. These were the hand-picked of an age, singled out by a process of Darwinian social selection, men best adapted for getting done those things that national survival required getting done. From the ethnologists also Ford derived his notion of England's fortuitous natural advantage over other nations in being always able to produce the required type. The secret lay in her extreme racial heterogeneity, which provided an infinite pool from which the forces of social selection might single out the particular dominant type demanded by the historical situation: "Somewhere in the back of our people, in the

11. *The Philosophy of History*, p. 370.
12. Taine, *History of English Literature*, p. 116.
13. Houston Stewart Chamberlain, *Foundations of the Nineteenth Century* (New York, 1912), I, 541.

great middle class, in the aristocracy, or in the submerged tenth, there are to be found men—the one man—fitted to deal with any emergency. And, if we consider our history and our composition as a people, we may find comforting assurance that this view is at least reasonably to be justified." [14] Here again Ford was simply pirating the commonplaces of social theorists like Herbert Spencer, whose facile jargon reflects the easy fusion of Darwinian process with Aryan myth:

Sundry instances point to the conclusion that a society formed from nearly-allied peoples of which the conquering eventually mingles with the conquered is relatively well fitted for progress. From their fusion results a community which, determined in its leading traits by the character common to the two, is prevented by their differences of character from being determined in its minor traits—is left capable of taking on new arrangements wrought by new influences: medium plasticity allows these changes of structure constituting advance in heterogeneity. . . . And our country, peopled by different divisions of the Aryan race, and mainly by varieties of Scandinavians, again illustrates this effect. . . .[15]

Despite the violence and mayhem Ford attributed to the age of feudalism, he saw it also as an age of extreme religious idealism, enjoying a sense of communalism in both commerce and religion such as the world has never since achieved. Credible or not, Ford always retained for his scheme a deep nostalgia, augmented by his awareness of the political and spiritual bankruptcy of the Edwardian scene: "We stand today, in the matter of political theories, naked to the wind and blind to the sunlight. We have a sort of vague uneasy feeling that the old feudalism and the old union of Christendom beneath a spiritual headship may in the end be infinitely better than anything that was ever devised by the Mother of Parliaments in England, the Constituent Assemblies in France, or all the Rules of the Constitution of the United States." [16]

14. Ford, *England and the English*, pp. 278–79.
15. Herbert Spencer, *The Principles of Sociology* (New York, 1896), I, 572–73.
16. Ford Madox Ford, *Henry James: A Critical Study* (New York, 1964), p. 47.

That same communal spirit, however, was fated to be shattered by the rapid growth of a spirit of individualism in the age to follow, an age Ford labeled the "Tudor-Stuart," stretching from approximately 1530 to 1688. The old feudal structure had cracked, then finally collapsed under the unrelenting pressure of Henry VII and the son who followed him. The brotherhood of great barons had crumbled first, after which men like Wolsey, Cromwell, and Cranmer had less trouble in bringing the Church to heel. The feudal dissolution sparked that period of painful transition, marked by a loosening of the old social and economic ties and a new spirit abroad in both politics and religion. The altered historical circumstances, the newly emergent *Zeitgeist*, argued Ford, called forth still another dominant type to replace the old, one best fitted to direct the nation's destiny both at home and abroad. For this new type, its hour come round at last, the idealism, altruism, and forthright action of the displaced medieval figure—these were no longer the peculiar variations demanded by the Time Spirit. They did, in fact, become distinct liabilities in this new historical cycle, ruled over by the image of Niccolo Machiavelli. For now, according to Ford, the winds of change were blowing directly from the palaces of the Medicis; and the Machiavellian representative of this spirit in England, Thomas Cromwell, was to have scant use for the directness, idealism, or altruism of the previous age:

Roughly speaking, the ideals of the [Tudor-Stuart] age that succeeded it [the feudal] were individualistic—opportunist. It was not, of course, England that was first in the field, since Italy produced Macchiavelli [*sic*]. But Italy, which produced Macchiavelli, failed utterly to profit by him. England, on the other hand, had to wait many years before falling into line with the spirit of its age. It had, as it were, to wait until most of the vested interest of the middle ages were got rid of—until practically the last of the great barons were brought to the ground.[17]

In a period where political duplicity and guile had become the current coin of the realm, it was the face and figure of Thomas

17. *England and the English*, p. 282.

Cromwell that stood out above all others in Ford's mind. Even against his own principles and convictions, Ford was openly fascinated by this lowborn son of a brewer who rose to become Lord Privy Seal of England during the reign of Henry VIII. Ford alludes favorably to Cromwell's memory in a number of books, but especially in *England and the English* and *The Critical Attitude*. It was the remorseless statecraft of Cromwell, that "cold scientist acting according to the maxims of Machiavelli," [18] that embodied for Ford the "spirit" of skepticism and opportunism that was to dominate the new age. Half angel, half devil, Cromwell delivered both Catholicism and the barony into the hands of the monarchy and fastened that Protestant spirit, continually wavering between statecraft and mercy, upon England for upwards of three hundred and fifty years, until its collapse in the reign of Edward VII.

Everywhere in Ford's discussion of this emerging type, one hears the whirring wheels of the Hegelian world machine picking, sorting, discarding, through that unique process of social selection, until England was able to "produce from its depths, from amidst its bewildering cross currents of mingled races, *the* great man of its age; and along with him, it produced a number of men similar in type, and strong enough to found a tradition." [19] From this tradition were to come such men as "the Cecils, the Wootons, the Bacons," men of practical politics, called forth in their turn by the forces of historical necessity, but no more aware of those forces than is the leaf of the wind that carries it along. Again the idea had begun with Hegel, who first suggested the way in which such World Historical Individuals could become the unconscious embodiment of the historical process: "Such individuals had no consciousness of the general idea they were unfolding, while prosecuting those aims of theirs; on the contrary, they were practical political men. But at the same time they were thinking men who had an insight into the requirements of the time—*what was ripe for development* [italics Hegel's]. This was

18. Ford Madox Ford, *The Critical Attitude* (London, 1911), p. 16.
19. *England and the English*, p. 283.

the very Truth for their age; for their world; the species next in order, so to speak." [20]

As I have said, however, it was not the direct influence of Hegel that lay behind Ford's historical thesis. It was instead a writer much closer to home, one who belonged to that school of British historians that had drawn most heavily upon the work of Hegel. This man was John Richard Green, whose *A Short History of the English People* revolutionized the entire approach to British history, both for Englishmen at large and for the young Ford studying at Praetoria House, an "advanced" boarding school in Folkestone. A student there from 1881 until his father's death in 1889, Ford was to vividly recall eighteen years later the powerful effect Green's *Short History* had made upon him as an impressionable boy of fifteen. The introduction of Green's text into the young Ford's history class had been a matter of general dismay. The consternation was occasioned by the fact that in both conception and presentation Green's approach was totally unique in the field of English history.

A brief examination today of Green's *Short History* is sufficient to indicate how it differed from all extant history texts of its day. Until its appearance in 1874, there was no competent modern survey of even the external facts of English history, though it was not merely with eternals or with the old "drum-and-trumpet" approach that Green was primarily concerned. "No existing history helped me," Green once wrote to a friend.[21] This was because no previous English historian had conceived of English history as an evolving national spirit. Perhaps Green's greatest break with traditional historicism lies in his rejection of historical divisions according to reigns or dynasties. Instead he sought to isolate the dominant governing feature of the day, the social and political *Zeitgeist* of the period, and afterwards to single out the individuals whose ideas and actions seemed most to epitomize their age. Green, in rejecting the historical

20. *The Philosophy of History*, p. 30.
21. Letter to J. Dawkins, September 11, 1862, in *Letters of John Richard Green*, ed. Leslie Stephen (London, 1901), p. 103.

approach then in vogue at Oxford, that of Ranke and the new school of "pragmatic" German historians, was coming closer to Renan's attempt to reconcile the achievement of individual historical figures, like Cromwell, with the collective achievement of their age. Avoiding the abstract analyses of Hume or the showy rhetoric of Macaulay, his nearest competitors, Green demonstrated the superior effectiveness of writing the sort of history recommended by Froude: "Wherever possible, let us not be told *about* this man or that. Let us hear the man himself speak; let us see him act, and let us be left to form our own opinions about him." [22] And so it is that Green's *Short History* abounds in recorded speeches of these "representative" historical figures. A close comparison of Ford's Tudor trilogy, particularly the speeches and sentiments of Thomas Cromwell, with Green's section on Tudor history will indicate how closely Ford was working from his old public-school text—or at least his memory of it.

These minutiae of Ford's indebtedness to Green are of less significance perhaps than that patterned and panoramic view the *Short History* suggested to the novelist. It was that sense of "process," of "a gradual and ordered growth" [23] that appealed to the pattern-seeker in Ford, and that he personally identified with the doctrines of Darwin. Ford recognized in Green what he called "the theory of evolution as applied to English history." [24] And though in later years Ford felt that the text had been pitched beyond the mental capabilities of himself and his schoolmates, he always insisted on the "sound theory" underlying the historian's revolutionary work. It was perhaps inevitable that Green's dramatization of English history should have instinctively appealed to Ford's precocious historical imagination, and that the young boy who was to become one of the ranking Impressionists of Edwardian fiction should have found in the vivid

22. J. A. Froude, "The Science of History," *Short Studies on Great Subjects* (New York, 1868), p. 34.
23. Ford, *England and the English*, p. 287.
24. *Ibid.*, p. 288.

scenes and speeches of Green's *Short History* those Hegelian contrasts and conflicts of social types that became the pattern for conflict in so many of his own novels.

Working from the patterns and historical events he gleaned from Green, and later from historical research of his own, Ford traced the birth and growth of the Tudor-Stuart period down to its subsequent decline in the face of a new historical age and the emergence of a new dominant psychological type. Of the declining Machiavellian figure he wrote: "This splendid and efficient dominant type had, of course, its apogee, its crest of the wave and its decline. It fell a little low with the second of the Stuart kings and, as far as international expression was concerned, its place was taken by the new, Puritan type." [25] With the inevitable circling of the years, each of Ford's historical-cultural ages, along with its dominant psychological type, was fated to give way before an ensuing historical epoch with a variant dominant type, a type better fitted to survive, even excel, in the altered historical milieu to follow. With the end of the Tudor-Stuart period there followed a third period whose initial phase was to provide the background for novels like *The "Half-Moon"* (1909) and *The Portrait* (1910).

At its inception this new age saw a still different dominant type come into its own, the Puritan. Germanic in race, pietistic in temperament, but commercially indefatigable, this figure had been an object of ridicule as late as the comedies of Shakespeare and Jonson. Within a generation, says Ford, the strain was ruling in England. After the brief and atavistic interlude of the Restoration, the type was firmly established in England with the Glorious Revolution of 1688 and the coronation of William of Orange as William III of England. This was the strain that was to hold sway down to the end of the nineteenth century, lending to that century its dominant national characteristics: ingenuousness, sentimentality, principle, and financial acumen. It is the breakdown of this third historical stage

25. *Ibid.,* p. 283.

that forms the setting for novels like *The Benefactor* (1905), *An English Girl* (1907), *A Call* (1920), *Mr. Fleight* (1913), and *The Good Soldier* (1915). Throughout this third cycle the trend towards individualism, as opposed to communalism, is intensified, moving England ever further from Ford's medieval ideal. It was not possible, according to Ford, to overestimate the influence of the Puritan mind, exemplified in the figure of William III, on the politics, religion, and art of subsequent British history. It was, argued Ford, simply everywhere; and it had led England directly into the dilemma it faced on the eve of the twentieth century:

. . . it lead the way for Walpole and the National Debt, and still holds us in its clutches. It did away with personal Royalty; it did away with priesthood; it did away very emphatically with the Arts, or rather, with the artistic spirit as a factor in life. . . . Philosophically speaking, too, it began that divorce of principle from life which . . . has earned for the English the title of a nation of hypocrites. It did this, of course, because it rivetted Protestantism for good and evil upon the nation's dominant types.[26]

By the last quarter of the nineteenth century the Puritan dynamic had dwindled away into that Philistine, dissenting temperament of which Arnold had warned: that bourgeois morality publicly impeccable and quietly deceitful, eternally vigilant to pillory the original moralist in its midst, which is the fate of older dominant types like Ashburnham, Tietjens, Moffat, and Kelleg.

Unwholesome as the dying period of this third historical cycle appeared to Ford, his apprehension was more strongly directed toward what would follow it. The new dominant psychological type, crudely allegorized in *The Inheritors*, seemed by contrast ruthless and unpitying, unconcerned with the Puritan tradition of principle, of individual liberty, rectitude, and grace—decadent though that tradition had become. As in the past, this new temperamental type was being called forth by environmental challenge, this time by the increasing commercial pressures from central Europe,

26. *Ibid.*, p. 290.

notably from Germany. To survive it would be necessary for England to approximate, even surpass what Ford termed the "Prussian mentality." The low esteem with which Ford regarded this mentality became later the subject of two entire books, *Between St. Dennis and St. George* (1915) and *When Blood Is Their Argument* (1915), and only part of his disapproval can be dismissed as the demands of wartime propaganda. Whether pose or persuasion, Ford's longtime criticism of the Prussian mind is scattered throughout his works, fiction and nonfiction alike. Again the influence of Green's anti-Teutonism may well have played its part. At any rate, British emulation of Prussian traits Ford deemed a betrayal of the whole Anglo-Saxon tradition. In many ways Ford early anticipated the coming of twentieth-century mass ideology with its brutal disregard for the individual.

Such were Ford's four ages of man. The struggle between these successive periods, during intervals of transition, became the stuff of dramatic conflict in all the better novels, both historical and contemporary, though even these latter become historical in a larger sense. There is one entire area of Ford's theory of successive psychological types that remains to be touched on. To each of his historical types Ford attributed distinctive physiognomic features; these in turn become a key to the psychological temperament of the particular character. Although *England and the English* contains the fullest description of the evolutionary process itself, it was a still earlier book, *Hans Holbein the Younger* (1905), that first suggested the direction Ford's historical imagination was to take. This book, a short monograph, was the by-product of research Ford had begun for a projected study of Henry VIII, abandoned when he discovered he had been anticipated by Pollard. Ford originally intended to illustrate this study "with reproductions of Holbein and the like." [27] Though much of this material was eventually incorporated into *The*

27. Ford Madox Ford, *Return to Yesterday* (New York, 1932), p. 168.

*Fifth Queen*, it first appeared in *Hans Holbein the Younger*, published by the Duckworth Press in 1905, part of a series on major European artists the Press was doing at the time. The over-all design of the series, under the general editorship of Arthur Strong, required that each of the artists be presented as exemplifying the dominant ideals and assumptions of his age.

More academic and less imaginative than Ford's *Holbein*, T. Sturge Moore's *Albert Dürer*,[28] another volume in the series, deals heavily with Dürer's life and art in its relationship to the age, but it lacks the historical perspective apparent in Ford's study. The approach laid down by Ford's editor, and the one the series followed, was that popularized by the school of "aesthetic historians" like Petrie in England, Alois Riegl in Germany, and Nikolas Danilevsky in Russia. The work of art itself is taken as an index to the state of the culture that produced it, an indication of sociocultural growth or decline, mute symbol of some historic *Zeitgeist* that might be reconstructed from the artistic productions of the age. Although Taine was thinking primarily of literature when he called cultural artifacts "a transcript of contemporary manners, a manifestation of a certain kind of mind," [29] the same claims were being made for the plastic arts. So Spengler, a later product of this tradition, searching zealously for symbols of decline, concentrated his attention on the plastic arts, particularly portraiture, proclaiming it to be "history captured in a moment." [30] After all, Ruskin had convinced the previous generation that the human countenance in portraiture was nothing less than the mirror of the soul.[31] And in Ford's own day the respected scientist Sir Francis Galton, in his *Inquiries into the Human Faculty*, had introduced what he thought a feasible method for evaluating facial expression as an index to human temperament

28. T. Sturge Moore, *Albert Dürer* (London, 1905).
29. *History of English Literature*, p. 1.
30. Oswald Spengler, *The Decline of the West* (New York, 1928), I, 101.
31. John Ruskin, *Modern Painters* (New York, 1889), II, 113.

and class differences. Little wonder that quack physiognomists were quick on the scene when the new Edward was crowned, eagerly searching his features for hopeful signs for the reign to come.[32]

Ford's physiognomic and psychological approach to history by way of the visual arts was then far less idiosyncratic than it might seem and had ample precedent in history, ethnology, and art criticism. Ford discusses Holbein's art as an expression of the prevailing world view of the artist's day. For purposes of historical and aesthetic comparison, he refers continually to the work of Dürer, which reflected, he said, a differing world view; that of the dying feudal period: "The two great artists are for the Germanic nations the boundary stones between the old world and the modern, between the old faith and the new learning, between empirical, charming conceptions of an irrational world and the modern theoretic way of looking at life. Dürer stood for the great imaginers who went before . . . the great feudal conceptions. Holbein commences the age of doubts, of merchants, of individual freedoms, of broader ideals, of an opening world and new hopes." [33]

In poring over the portraits of Holbein and Dürer, Ford caught in those faces a glimpse of a changing world order, similar to that which had been suggested in Green's *Short History*. Two years later while outlining his concept of English history, he described his dominant Tudor-Stuart type by recalling the faces he had studied in the Holbein paintings, particularly the Windsor group: "The dominant type of the Tudor-Stuart ages presents itself to me as dark, bearded and shrewd." [34] By contrast, said Ford, the Dürer paintings depicted an earlier, totally different physical type—that of the medieval figure: "The life which Dürer's art seems to close was an out-of-door life, or at least it was a life that was passed outside of

32. "The Queen," February 2, 1901, as quoted in James Laver, *Edwardian Promenade* (Boston, 1958), p. 16.
33. Ford Madox Ford, *Hans Holbein the Younger: A Critical Monograph* (Chicago and New York, 1914), p. 9.
34. *England and the English*, p. 289.

great cities. His lords ride hunting in full steel from small castles on ragged . . . looking crags. . . . The flesh of his figures is hardened, dried, and tanned by exposure to the air. . . ." [35] Dürer's physical types, fitted into the historical pattern suggested by Green, became the archetypes for Ford's re-creation of medieval characters—violent, out-of-doors men, ruddy of complexion, but nevertheless activated by religious idealism: "Dürer was a mystic, the last fruit of a twilight of the gods. In his portraits, the eyes dream, accept, or believe in the things they see." [36] Ford's reconstruction of this type reflects as well the mythologizing of the pan-Germanic ethnologists at work during these years tracing the first flowering of the so-called Teutonic genius. Houston Stewart Chamberlain had described the type with its "great radiant heavenly eyes . . . the gigantic stature, the symmetrical muscular development . . . the lofty countenance, required by an elevated spiritual life." [37] Consequently, Ford's association of muscularity, violence, and religious altruism was part of the popular ethnological folklore of the Edwardian scene and in no way original with him. What was original was Ford's belief in the inexorable process of evolutionary historicism, which made the disappearance of such a type inevitable. In fact, in Dürer's own time this type, and the World Spirit it epitomized, was already on the wane, slated to be displaced by that new variation in the species, the Tudor Machiavellian.

This new wave, argued Ford, already rolling over Europe in Holbein's time, was everywhere evident in the artist's canvases. They represented, Ford concluded, not only a different racial stock (the "Italian-Celtic") but an absolute alteration in physique and physiognomy, a reflection not solely of their individual temperaments but of an altered climate of opinion wafted in by the Renaissance: "Holbein's lords no longer ride hunting. They are inmates of palaces, their flesh is rounded, their limbs at rest, their eyes sceptical

35. *Hans Holbein*, pp. 11–12.
36. *Ibid.*, p. 13.
37. *Foundations*, I, 535.

or contemplative. They are indoor statesmen; they deal in intrigues; they have already learnt the meaning of the words, "The balance of the Powers," and in consequence they wield the sword no longer; they have become sedentary rulers." [38] These, in Ford's historical panorama, become the followers of Machiavelli: men indigent, corpulent, cunning—masters in the new art of statecraft. The deviousness centered in their eyes was to become very nearly a leit-motif in the Katherine Howard novels. Ford was to postulate the physical characteristics of still another, a third, dominant type: the post Tudor-Stuart figure who dominated the English scene from approximately 1688 down to the end of the nineteenth century: a type tall, fair-haired, blue-eyed and "hard featured," Germanic by racial origin. In short, this was the Puritan of whom I shall say more in the summary below. Near the close of *England and the English*, Ford alludes briefly to a new emerging type in his day—a figure short and dark of hue, unquestionably a reference to the increasing prominence of the Jew in Edwardian society. It is this figure who struggles with the atavistic medievalist Blood in *Mr. Fleight*, but Ford was very sketchy in his commentary and description of this last type, contenting himself with merely a temperamental description, and even this was to vary at times.

Summarized briefly, Ford's outline of history shows four successive stages in the development of the English peoples. As these stages succeed one another through history, important alterations are observable in five important areas: (1) the dominant psychological type, (2) the physique and physiognomy of this type, (3) the racial background, (4) the religious orientation of the age, and (5) the socioeconomic and political structure of the period. No single period represents a water-tight historical epoch, but together they represent Ford's four ages of English man.

The "pre-Tudor" age encompasses the period from approximately the eleventh century down to 1500, though Ford is hazy about its

38. *Hans Holbein*, p. 12.

exact genesis. About its racial stock, there is no uncertainty; it is "French-Norman," yielding a dominant physical type "rufous, reddish tanned" with "dusky red complexions," the result of constant exposure to the elements. Theirs was the age of the great barons, high-stomached men blown with restless violence around their turbulent times, quicker to strike than to parley, ready to parley only when spent. Still they were men whose eyes might behold the Holy Grail, altruists and idealists who could, with no sense of paradox, pay allegiance to both the chivalric code and Roman Catholicism alike. As examples of this type Ford singles out historical figures like the Black Prince, Du Guesclin in France, and the third Earl of Norfolk. Ford's description of Norfolk's face and figure in the Holbein monograph is the first glimpse of a human and historical situation that becomes the key to Ford's peculiar family of heroes—that vestigial dominant type who has lived on into an uncongenial historical environment where he inevitably comes to grief: "And was it not that bitter, soured, and disappointed Duke of Norfolk whom Holbein painted like a survival from the olden times, standing up rigid and unbending in a new world that seemed to him a sea of errors. . . ?"[39] Both scene and situation were to be reproduced almost exactly in *The Fifth Queen*, although it is Norfolk's niece, Katherine Howard, who becomes the fullest dramatic representation of this figure, Ford's alien protagonist whose struggle and failure amidst the uncertain moral terrain of a later age becomes an indictment of that age.

Ford's second age, the Tudor-Stuart period, stretching from 1500 to 1688, is really a transition period between the medieval and modern world, although it did produce its own dominant type, embodying the unique character of the age. The racial stock of this figure, says Ford, is "Italian-Celtic," resulting in a "heavy, dark, bearded, bull-necked animal . . . with devious and twinkling eyes," torsos rounded, fleshy and inert—by contrast with the lithe, hard-

39. *Ibid.*, p. 14.

ened musculature of the medieval figures. These are the Tudor Machiavellians, suited by temperament to gain ascendancy in a historical period characterized by guile and duplicity. By nature skeptical and opportunistic, they triumph easily over the medieval figures in any public confrontation, their battleground the king's council room and darkened passageways rather than the sunny fields of medievalism. As opportunists their religious affiliation is *either* Catholic or Lutheran depending on the prevailing wind from the royal bedchamber. The political and social situation, inextricable from the religious conflict, exists in a state of turmoil although the power center has shifted from the barons to the crown, worn now by Henry VIII. This monarch's trimming between England past and England future makes him the ideal ruler for an age of intrigue, peopled with Machiavellian counsellors like Thomas Cromwell.

But this dominant type was fated in turn to be superseded by a still later variation: the Puritan, who first gravitates to power after the "Bloodless Revolution" of 1688, though the type had begun to appear by the close of Elizabeth's reign. Germanic in racial origins, physically it was tall, fair-haired, and "hard featured." A "not very splendid" type, it represents a new evolutionary development of the English national spirit. Ingenuous, unimaginative, and sentimental, its forte lies in pious frugality and thrift, as well as commercial shrewdness, always a reflection of God's grace. Possessed of a Protestant ethic, humanly unattainable in Ford's view, it has necessary recourse to hypocrisy to disguise its inevitable failure to live up to its impossible ideals. Neither the field of combat nor the council room represents its domain, but the counting house. Thrown into conflict with the crude, unthinking vigor of the medieval figures, it overcomes by its infuriating shrewdness, as witness the bafflement of Edward Colman in The *"Half-Moon."* When confronted by the unprincipled secularism of the Tudor-Stuart, it triumphs through appeal to moral disapprobation, an atmosphere unfamiliar to the Machiavellian and under which he cannot operate. Philistine in its smug contempt of the arts, dissenting in its religiosity, this Puritan mentality, argued Ford, was to form the English national character up until the close of the nineteenth century, when it begins to fade before a new psychological shift.

Such a shift could well seem propitious to the more vigorous advocates of progress like Wells, men acutely conscious of the negative aspects of Victoria's reign. The alternative to many seemed a necessary ruthlessness so that Richard Remington, the leader of the "Young Imperialist" movement in Wells's *The New Machiavelli*, spoke for many in his generation when he denounced "the slackness, mental dishonesty, presumption, mercenary respectability and sentimentalized commercialism of the Victorian period," and called for a more vigorous approach to the problems of the day. This attitude, coupled with the mounting commercial and military pressure of central Europe, argued Ford, was leading England toward a vital alteration of its national spirit: one that was harsh, uncompassionate, unsentimental, contemptuous of principles or idealism, dubious of individual human worth, and committed to the sacrifice of the individual for the good of the state—in short, a blanket repudiation of traditional English values. This, Ford feared, was the direction the World Spirit was now taking, and if England were to survive in the struggle for existence she must fight the world with the world's weapons. To their credit, many of Ford's twentieth-century protagonists, vestigial relics of an earlier Time Spirit, find the cost of survival too high and end their days as failures like Kelleg, suicides like Ashburnham, or recluses like Christopher Tietjens.

These were the four successive dominant English types which had, in turn, both controlled and symbolized their respective historical periods from the death of Harold to the coronation of Edward VII. In Ford's historical ethnology these psychological types are permanently fixed and occur in all ages. Depending on historical circumstances, what Hegel had called the "Time Spirit," different types will be called to the fore at various times. Other types, as it were, go underground for a period awaiting the next turn of "humanity's wheel," as the god Apollo calls it in *Mr. Apollo.* If, however, they choose to oppose the prevailing Time Spirit, they are invariably ground down before the social dynamics of Ford's historical cyclicalism. It is because these variant types can and do appear in any age that one finds those peculiar physical and temperamental resemblances scattered all through Ford's novels, even among secondary characters. It is why Lady Blanche, in *Ladies Whose Bright Eyes*, set in the fifteenth century, resembles Lord Aldington of *The New Humpty-Dumpty*, set in the twentieth century, who in turn has the physiognomy and temperament of Henry VIII in *The Fifth Queen*, sixteenth century, as well as of Henry Hudson of *The "Half-Moon,"* with its seventeenth-century setting. Although such comparisons yield little in themselves, it becomes increasingly clear that Ford's continual and heavy practice of detailed character description was not simply impressionistic canon, nor even Conrad's determination "to make you see," but the visual and psychological expression of his substrative theory of historical, psychological, and ethnological evolution.

Whatever Ford's worth as a critic of society or as a student of history, he was admittedly no systematic thinker and there are, as one might expect, howling irregularities in his judgments on history and society. His bitter denunciation of public ferocity in support of the Boer War sits uneasily alongside his nostalgic admiration for a medieval England where violence was the order of the day. The only discernible difference seems to have been the religious leavening in the medieval period, which somehow renders violence less reprehensible. Equally indefensible, from the historian's point of view, is that cavalier lumping of both Tudor and Stuart monarchs in the same Machiavellian bin as shrewd, calculating rulers. The demonstrated monarchic incompetence of nearly the whole Stuart line hardly resembles the politic statecraft of Elizabeth, or of her father or her grandfather.

Nor did Ford, in assigning psychological implications to the Holbein and Dürer paintings, make allowance for clear differences in technique and conception. Ford, working deductively, singled out canvases that supported his *a priori* theories lifted almost in their entirety from Green's *Short History*. Certainly it would be difficult to find a countenance more unlike Ford's medieval ideal than the shrewd, piercing skepticism of Dürer's *Hans Imhof*. Ford was guilty of an assumption that, as Lukács has pointed out, characterized most of the art-historical theories of the Edwardian period—that "the thoughts, feelings and motives of present-day men" are similar to those of the past.[40] In part Ford's error came from the historical assumptions implicit in Green's *Short History*, that such cultural contrasts could be made and were a valid part of historical conjecture. Whatever the contradictions in Ford's historical prospect, they are those of the imaginative artist intent on finding some broader pattern of meaning for his criticism of the contemporary scene. And whatever his assumptions about historical and ethnological development, they are those shared by the men of his day.

Granting Ford's assumption of an evolving British personality, one still faces the question of why Ford belongs to the regressive rather than the progressive school of evolutionary thought. Why did he choose to align himself with the doomsters rather than the yea-sayers? True, the Boer War is the ostensible reason he cites and it might not be necessary to look beyond that, but any age—and especially the Edwardian—presents sufficient multiplicity to justify either optimism or pessimism. As we have seen, general theories of decline were no more prevalent among artists than were those of hopefulness—that peculiar Alpha-Omega complex I have noted. There was, of course, the influence of Conrad's Slavic melancholy during the crucial period of collaboration on *The Inheritors;* and Conrad's gloomy view of history as well as of the contemporary scene may well have played a part in shaping Ford's own depression. But there is another, a more immediate and earlier influence, earlier even than Ford's reading of Green's *A Short History of the English People*. This was Ford's own father, the scholar and critic Dr. Franz Hueffer.

Ford's few allusions to his father reflect only the awe and respect

40. Georg Lukács, *The Historical Novel* (Boston, 1963), p. 176.

elicited by a slightly forbidding parent whose rule over his children was both absolute and unquestioned. Nowhere does Ford acknowledge his father's views on evolution and history as an influence of his own mental development, but there is a self-evident similarity—in both temperament and idea. Whatever that "tinge of melancholy" Goldring noted in Ford's father, or that description of him as "a hypochondriacal duffer" in Dante Gabriel Rossetti's well-known limerick, these things are of lesser import than Dr. Hueffer's own deep preoccupation with the writings of Schopenhauer. Like H. G. Wells after him, he regarded Schopenhauer's doctrine of the evolving will as an anticipation of Darwinism. And from those two seminal nineteenth-century minds, the elder Hueffer went on to formulate his own vision of those successive types doomed to extinction in the forward rush of an amoral history: "Everywhere we see struggle for existence, species devouring species, race contending against race. . . . Surely this is not a bright picture, and Schopenhauer has painted it with the sombrest hues of despair. He lays bare the revolting cruelty of Nature, which at the cost of inconceivable individual suffering creates new types only to abandon them again to the universal doom of destruction." [41] The melancholy note of *fin de siècle* despair was never so heavy in the son, but there is the same assumption of process and an inevitable dark destiny permeating Ford's view of the history upon which his novels are based. And that assumption was in many ways the cornerstone he and Conrad chose for their art: "Before everything a story much convey a sense of inevitability: that which happens in it must seem to be the only thing that could have happened. . . . The problem of the author is to make his then action the only action that character could have taken. It must be inevitable, because of his character, because of his ancestry . . . or on account of the gradual coming together of the thousand small circumstances by which Destiny, who is inscrutable and august, will push us into one certain predicament." [42]

41. Francis Hueffer, *Musical Studies* (Edinburgh, 1880), pp. 121–22.
42. Ford Madox Ford, *Joseph Conrad: A Personal Remembrance* (New York, 1965), pp. 218–19.

That "Destiny" that dogs the heels of Ford's protagonists becomes less "inscrutable" when viewed against the background of the father's Schopenhauerean gloom and Ford's own concept of historical determinism. The best of the novels from 1901 to 1915 reflect Ford's variant attempts to render implicitly the human consequences of such a pattern in the movement of history, though the basic formula was to remain unchanged. This consisted of taking a dominant historical type from one historical period and placing him in the alien and hostile world of a different age. Here the protagonist's very strengths become debilitating weaknesses, driving him toward relentless self-destruction. Consequently, it is incorrect to argue, as a recent critic has, that Ford learned only late in life that all essential conflict must be between man's essential nature and social convention.[43] Such a pattern was there almost from the beginning and its deterministic nature reflects in the Edwardian mind that increasing awareness of the absolute beggardom of the doctrine of free will. And though Ford was a Catholic of sorts, within his fictive universe his protagonists are never the captains of their fate. Quite the contrary. Given Ford's conviction in the inevitability of human actions, free will is not so much inoperative as it is an agency of self-destruction presided over by a slightly ironic and Hardyesque god.

If the historical assumptions underlying Ford's relentless antagonism between man and social milieu seem unduly Daedalian, their operation within the novels is by contrast simple and effective—the inevitable and predetermined failure of protagonists like Katherine Howard, Edward Colman, Edward Ashburnham, and Christopher Tietjens. After all, the basic formula for the tragic hero in all of literature is essentially unvaried; he is, as Northrop Frye has said, "somebody who gets isolated from his society." [44] It was for Ford to define anew in his own age how that isolation might be artistically embodied in terms most meaningful to his times.

43. R. W. Lid, "Tietjens in Disguise," *Kenyon Review*, XXII (Spring, 1960), 276.
44. Norhtrop Frye, *Anatomy of Criticism* (Princeton, N.J., 1957), p. 41.

The suffusion of popularized notions of evolutionary and racial process in the art, history, and philosophy of the day provided him with that mythical construct, deterministic in its working, that broods over all his major protagonists. Born out of their proper time slot they all suffer the effects of moral and psychological dislocation. Some few, like Don Kelleg and Robert Grimshaw, are able to adapt sufficiently to survive. Others, like Katherine Howard, Edward Colman, and Edward Ashburnham, are physically destroyed. In a few of the early novels—notably *A Call, Ladies Whose Bright Eyes,* and *Mr. Fleight*—the protagonist is able to survive in the particular society through a growth in self-knowledge under the aegis of some compatible woman. There is a discernible connection between this problem of self-knowledge and Ford's theory of domniant psychological types, especially in the novels written between 1905 and 1911, although the pattern is still there in later novels such as *The Rash Act* (1933) and *Henry for Hugh* (1934). And as late as 1930 Ford was still relying on racial and evolutionary theories developed earlier to explain the predatory business executive Joe Notterdam, whose vestigial instincts and physical type represent a throwback to an earlier age of violence and barbarity. But by this time the pattern of Ford's earlier and better novels has grown faint and there are only isolated echoes.

The real stuff of tragedy had come earlier when a Katherine Howard seeks to impose her medievalistic and Dürer-like spirit on an alien Tudor world. It was while writing *The Fifth Queen,* his first historical novel, that Ford first employed that pattern of conflict—a conflict based on his historical mythos—that he later transferred to the modern scene. Disappointment over *The Inheritors,* with its fabulistic explanation of an altering national psychology, convinced Ford of the need for greater aesthetic distance in dealing with historical phenomena. At any rate, later in his career he was to insist that "the creative artist is almost always an expatriate and almost always writes about the past. He *must,* in order to get perspective, retire both in space and time from the model upon

which he is at work." [45] For a writer in the new century such
retirement was more mandatory than ever before. Traditional modes
of belief in the Edwardian era were unraveling at an appalling rate
and the artist found himself increasingly cut off from that ground of
common assumption that artist and audience had once mutually
enjoyed. By retreating from the contemporary scene to an earlier
age of historical flux, Ford gradually developed that technique he
would later use in depicting the modern scene: the dramatic conflict
between the prevailing spirit of the age and a protagonist exemplifying the Time Spirit of an earlier age. As a device of social criticism, it
is another variation on the "alien eye" technique, Ford's personal
and original means of defining the problems of a faltering Edwardian society.

Hence that oft-noted similarity in Ford's protagonists that has
fascinated critics, and the inevitable fate society metes out to them.
To label them "altruists," "Christian gentlemen," or "romantic idealists" is to overemphasize their personal and temperamental resemblances. Their kinship is situational, not temperamental, which is
where previous criticism has erred. Their common root lies in
Ford's assumption of a psychological evolution within a deterministic system of world history, none the less pervasive for its artistic
concealment. Once Ford had shaped that system in the Katherine
Howard novels, it became the coign of vantage from which he
descended with increasing sureness of flight into the contemporary
scene. In both his historical novels and those set in the present, it is
the fittest who survive, not the finest; and the fittest are determined
by the peculiar demands of successive historical periods that call
forth different dominant types. Such was Ford's "ruling theory."

45. Ford Madox Ford, *Mightier Than the Sword* (London, 1938), p. 207.

# 3. The Tudor Trilogy

A basic ground rule for any study of Ford is the need to disentangle his achievement from his own commentary on that achievement, for few novelists have seemed so perverse and arbitrary in their self-analysis. Maddeningly self-contradictory as are all of Ford's mendacious memoirs, nowhere has he thrown up so much dust as with his work in the historical novel. The worst of the lot, *The Young Lovell*, he once described in a letter to his agent as a "big and serious historical work rather like *The Fifth Queen*." [1] An obvious attempt to arouse his agent's waning interest, the statement is outrageously false, for the novel does not come within a country mile of the Tudor novel —as Ford well knew. In still a different mood, Ford could turn his back on the entire genre, proclaiming that "with me the historical novel was always and almost of necessity a *tour de force*," [2] exactly the phrase and sentiment he had used seven years earlier in labeling

1. Letter to J. B. Pinker dated March 17, 1913, in *Letters of Ford Madox Ford*, ed. Richard M. Ludwig (Princeton, N.J., 1965), p. 56.
2. Ford Madox Ford, *Return to Yesterday* (New York, 1932), p. 284.

his historical fiction "a fake." [3] And a fake it might seem if one accepted as well his spurious recollection that "all the notes I ever made for my historical novels were contained on the backs of three or four visiting cards and then were only dates." [4]

Although such cavalier dismissal might seem to make Ford's achievement in *The Fifth Queen* even more impressive, it belies the extended research Ford had undertaken for his proposed history of Henry VIII, material subsequently incorporated into the Katherine Howard novels. That Ford disliked writing historical novels both his early letters and late reminiscence testify, as well as that silent anger he once directed at Dr. Garnett of the British Museum for first suggesting he might turn his hand to a historical novel—or perhaps "something on pirates." Despite Ford's mute outrage, the Tudor novels were to become his most popular, while *Romance*, his "pirate" story, eventually found its way to Hollywood.

Ford's misleading, often cavalier, statements about his historical novels have encouraged critics to undervalue their importance, both in themselves and in their role in shaping Ford's approach to novels set in Edwardian society. Whatever Ford's personal feeling about the genre, history had been a lifelong passion and—in some ways— his most persistent subject. There was a time before the Pollard disappointment and the sorry debacle of "small producerism" at Pent cottage when he visualized a life as "country gentleman-historian." Unfortunately the arrival on the world scene of his special bugbear, the "age of the specialist," precluded this. And he realized, as Pater had before him, that if one pursues an "impressionistic" rendering of history, then the whole guise of historicism must be dropped, and one can claim to be no more than a romancer. And yet was anything else possible? As eminent a critic of the historical novel as Brander Matthews said not, reflecting Edwardian historians'

3. Ford Madox Ford, *Joseph Conrad: A Personal Remembrance* (New York, 1965), p. 176.
4. Ford, *Return to Yesterday*, p. 284.

own despair at re-creating the past. If, as he wrote in 1901, one cannot really know "how the people of those days did feel and think and act," [5] how can one make a pretense of writing a valid historical novel? Ford was fully sensible of the dilemma when describing his own problems with the historical novel:

The business of all novelists is to trick you into believing you have taken part in the scenes that they render. But the historical novelist is on the horns of a dilemma: he must either present you with the superficial view of history given by the serious and scientific historian than whom no one is more misleading, or diving deeper he must present you with the mendacities in which mankind perforce indulges when treating of contemporary events or its immediate fellows. For who are we to know the truth? [6]

Fortunately the solipsistic tendency among even genuine historians was to give the artist all the license he could ask. And Conrad, speaking for himself—as well as for Ford and James—went on to suggest that the contemporary Edwardian novelist had become of necessity a historian: "Fiction is history, human history, or it is nothing. But it is also more than that; it stands on firmer ground, being based on the reality of forms and the observation of social phenomena, whereas history is based on documents . . . on second-hand impression." [7] In trying to cope with what seemed an increasingly incomprehensible universe, the arts demanded the same permissiveness of interpretation the sciences were allowing themselves. Insofar as the old and popular notion of Truth Absolute had developed what Ford called "the bewildering faculty of the chameleon," the artist—especially one mindful of Zolaesque canon—felt increasingly justified in manipulating ideas and events in an effort to impose some meaningful pattern on human activity.

Writing to John Galsworthy, Conrad once described Ford's *The*

5. Brander Matthews, *The Historical Novel: and Other Essays* (New York, 1901), p. 8.
6. Ford Madox Ford, "Dedication" to *A Little Less than Gods* (New York, 1928), p. viii.
7. Joseph Conrad, *Notes on Life and Letters* (London, 1925), p. 20.

*Fifth Queen* as "a noble conception—the swan song of Historical Romance." [8] "Swan song" suggests that dwindling popularity that Matthews, some years earlier, had noted in the fortunes of the historical novel. And yet Maurice Hewlett alone, from 1898 to 1901, had produced four historical novels all set in the two ages Ford was to contrast in *The Fifth Queen*. And the military romance, which included historical novels, had been the conspicuous favorite of more than a generation of late Victorian readers. Although the term "historical romance" suggests a more exotic subject matter than simply "historical novel," the distinction is somewhat more complex —especially in an age when the novel itself was rapidly replacing poetry as the favorite vehicle for social commentary. Consequently it is necessary to review briefly the major developments in the British historical novel during the half century just before Ford's career. In addition to clarifying the form the genre had taken by the eighteen-seventies, the discussion should make clear that although Ford belongs in the mainstream of this tradition, his more deliberate concept of history raises his work above even his most illustrious predecessors—writers like Scott, Bulwer-Lytton, and Stevenson.

Traditionally the historical novel had dealt with greater or lesser historical personages of brief or prolonged appearance and had been written in a spirit of serious scholarship. In this manner the historical novelist had sought to suggest the flavor of the age. The conception, if not the form, of the genre saw its genesis in the Waverley novels of Scott. Both his settings and his dramatization of historical conflict became that which he described in his successive prefaces and introductions: the clash of two historical cultures in an age of transition. His conflicts were embodied in characters drawn from the two ages—the one disappearing, the other aborning: and always they embodied the dominant character of their respective ages. Their struggles represent history taken at the level of the individual

---

8. Letter to John Galsworthy dated February 20, 1908, in Jean-Aubry, *Joseph Conrad: Life and Letters* (New York, 1927), II, 67.

or, as Conrad put it, "human history." *Ivanhoe, Redgauntlet,* and *The Monastery* were all constructed along these lines; and they set the pattern for the remainder of the nineteenth century. And though the fundamental formula remained essentially unaltered through Victoria's reign, there came that interim and predictable moral emphasis in the historical novels of Bulwer-Lytton, particularly in *Harold, The Last of the Barons,* and the early *Rienzi*. Practice might vary slightly from author to author or critic to critic concerning to what extent one should permit the entrance of recognizable historical personages and events. Scott's own approach, to judge by *Kenilworth* and *Ivanhoe,* was flexible. But for the most part he preferred, unlike Ford or Bulwer-Lytton, to place recognizable historical personages at a distance from the central action. These matters aside, there was the unstated assumption that the author would reproduce as accurately as possible the essential flavor of the times.

That Clio and Calliope should have been sister muses gives mythic testimony to the long and close association between the two disciplines. Yet the historical novel as we know it today could not come into being until the early nineteenth century when there began to emerge a systematic and formalized view of history itself. Until then Clio's had been a mantle of shreds and patches. Even Froude's relatively modern and dramatized historical commentary bore the marks of his genius for disorganization—with those dartings backwards and forwards in time hardly less bewildering than those of *The Good Soldier*. Scott's seminal position in the historical novel is in part the result of mere historical happenstance. His vogue as a poet eclipsed by the rising popularity of the young Byron, Scott turned to the novel as the Napoleonic era was edging toward Waterloo. Had he accomplished nothing else, Napoleon made history a "mass experience" and the age of Scott acutely aware of contemporary history on the move. The two previous decades had witnessed more major historical events than had the previous two hundred years and had awakened speculation over the possibility of some discernible pattern in the movement of history. For example, the very success of Napoleon's armies themselves had called into existence their antithesis—a European coalition that would have been unthinkable thirty years earlier. And England herself was often singled out as a clear and isolated example of unmistakable historical process with its unequivocal, if spasmodic, movement towards a constitutional monarchy.

It was Hegel, of course, who first summed up in *The Philosophy of History* the speculations of nineteenth-century historicism. By reconciling the ideas of Kant, Fichte, Herder, and Schelling, he gave a new explanation of the direction and mechanics of historical process. In moving towards its ultimate end of human moral freedom, Hegel's peculiarly schizoid "World Spirit" lurches first left, then right in its phoenix passage through time: "It [the World Spirit] certainly makes war upon itself—consumes its own existence; but in this very destruction it works up that existence into a new form, and each successive phase becomes in turn a material working on which it exalts itself to a new grade." [9] The mechanics of process in Hegelian thought, with its obvious implications of "progress," was to play into the hands of glib Victorian historians like Macaulay, who chose to become apologists for the industrial momentum of the late nineteenth century. But it had its influence as well on more serious and reflective historians like Green and the entire Oxford School. Unquestionably there was an innate hopefulness in Hegelianism that clearly suggested an improving world order arising phoenix-like from yesteryear. Although Hegel never underestimated the suffering in those conflagrations of history that seared old traditions while tempering the new, his mystic and romantic mind was ever filled with images, not only of the legendary phoenix but of those oriental doctrines of metempsychosis as well.

Though Walter Scott as far as we know never read Hegel, his

9. Georg Wilhelm Friedrich Hegel, *The Philosophy of History*, trans. J. Sibree (New York, 1956), p. 73.

novels are a remarkable anticipation of the German philosopher's ideas. And it is the pattern of conflict in the Waverley novels that is unmistakably stamped upon the plot and dramatic structure of the historical novel as it was to develop during the remainder of the nineteenth century. The resolution of those conflicts between cultures in all of Scott's major historical novels was that proverbial English *via media* between contending social forces.

It was that recurrent element of strife and conflict that made Hegel's theories so applicable to the fiction of the historical novelist, so that even where those theories were not known, as with Scott, their fictional counterpart was inevitably called into being by that necessity for social conflict demanded of the genre. Fichte, for example, for whom history was a relatively smooth and uninterrupted flow, was of no use whatsoever to writers of historical fiction. Despite the emphasis on social conflict in Scott's novels, the author of *Waverley* seldom turned this conflict toward contemporary social criticism, despite the tremendous social dislocations and public unrest following the close of the Napoleonic wars. Such application had to await the unexceptional experimentation of Scott's major successor, Edward George Bulwer-Lytton, and—a generation later—the more nearly consummate artistry of Ford Madox Ford.

In his disinterest with social criticism, Scott exists outside the mainstream of the English novel stretching from Richardson to the present; and for this he has been severely indicted by Muir and others. Still such criticism partially ignores the permutations the novel was undergoing in Scott's time: the return to the romance, a tradition that was to culminate in the period of Ford's early experimentation nearly a century later. As early as the Waverley novels the distinction had arisen between the novel and the romance in novel form. The novel was characterized by a higher degree of "realism" in character and incident, while the romance was typified by a far greater reliance upon the novelist's invention. And the projection of one's personal views of life and history like that implicit in Ford's early novels was gradually accepted as an integral part of the romance. Certainly the Waverley novels bear the unmistakable imprint of Scott's own personal projection of historical process: the belief that even the most bitter social, economic, political, and religious struggles have always settled down to that equitable "middle way," so that out of the conflict of Saxon and Norman comes the increased tolerance and understanding of Richard and Cedric the Saxon toward each other by the end of *Ivanhoe*. Scott's greatest achievement was to give a sense of historicity and dignity to the previously suspect genre of the romance. By combining the respectability of history and direct observation with that sense of wonder drawn from the old romance he secured a place for the new form; and, more importantly, he gave to the historical romance that essential form that was to persist down through the Edwardian era.

The essence of the Waverley novels lay in the continual tension wrought by the conflict of cultural opposites. Scott was, as Leslie Stephen once said, "the first imaginative observer who saw distinctly how the national type of character is the product of past history, and embodies all the great social forces by which it has slowly shaped itself." [10] Like Ford, Scott saw this "national type" as one that had undergone continual evolution from a violent, heroic past down to the age of prudence and unheroic circumspection. Consequently, the central conflict in both *Redgauntlet* and *The Fifth Queen* is a struggle between a vital, heroic, and wrongheaded past and a more prudential and calculating present. Hence comes that discernible "flatness" noted by the critics in both Ford's and Scott's heroes. That is, they are already completed characters when they arrive on the scene, their historical psychologies a *fait accompli*. With the possible exception of Katherine Howard, none of Ford's characters develops psychologically, and Katherine does only because Ford sensed, upon finishing the first novel, the insufficiency of

10. Leslie Stephen, *Hours in a Library* (New York, 1927), I, 224.

her motivation, which he then moved to rectify in the concluding two novels. But in Ford's later protagonists there is no real development; it is at most vacillation. Being the paradigms of a particular historical *Zeitgeist*, his heroes, like Scott's, are essentially complete at the outset.

Scott was more sanguine than Ford about the superiority of the modern world over the ancient and medieval, so that where the resolutions of his plots represent a victory of order over temporary chaos, the resolutions of Ford's novels usually result in another defeat for those splendid but outmoded human types that figure as his protagonists. Subsequently for Scott the outcome of this historical conflict was always an index of that sure, if limited, advance in human progress that comprised the center of his historical assumptions. In Ford's novels, the failure of the protagonist becomes an implicit criticism of that "modern" spirit that has usurped the old ways. Though they were to interpret variously the end toward which history was bending, Scott and Ford are remarkably similar in their views on the mechanics of history; and these views were to shape the dramatic structures of their works. It is, however, easy to exaggerate the similarity in the dilemmas facing their romantic heroes, and even more to assume that with Scott most of his heroes are thin carbon copies of one another—exactly the same mistake that critics have made with Ford. In fact an early reviewer in the *Edinburgh Review* commented upon the "strong fraternal likeness" in Scott's major characters. It was inevitable perhaps that both Scott and Ford should have suffered from this sort of misreading; but what the critics of both were mistaking for character similarity was really a situational similarity—one in which their various heroes represent obsolete cultural and ethical values, having survived on into an uncongenial society. And yet the situation is always less critical for a Cedric or a Quentin Durward than it is for an Edward Colman or a Katherine Howard, who die—bitter, alone, and isolated. Their plight is more that described by Mario Praz in *The Hero in Eclipse:* unregenerate rebels against society, refusing to capitulate or accept. History, in this sense, was always kinder to Scott's relics than to Ford's.

So although both Scott and Ford wrote their historical fiction from a strongly Hegelian point of view, as far as the mechanics of change was concerned, Ford evinces none of that Hegelian optimism that permeates Scott's work. Ford, more fundamentally the artist, was primarily concerned with individual fate rather than with the abstract possibility of some eventual good accruing to the mass of mankind. As a result his histories deal with the tragedy and failure of individuals rather than with the success of historical idealism. Such a complacent idealism permitted Scott to raise his eyes above the social injustice of his day, while Ford, closer to Scott's successor Bulwer-Lytton in this respect, found in the historical novel a path that led directly to a social criticism of the contemporary world.

Bulwer-Lytton, whose first historical novel, *The Last Days of Pompeii*, appeared two years after the death of Scott, provides a convenient link between the historical romance of Scott's day and that of Ford's. Bulwer-Lytton was openly critical of Scott's avoidance of ethical and philosophical concerns in the Waverley novels. In fact, Scott's sensibilities seemed to fall deplorably short of Bulwer-Lytton's more highly developed and Victorian moral sensitivity. Consequently *Rienzi* (1835), *The Last of the Barons* (1843), and *Harold* (1848) were an attempt at turning history to the purposes of moral edification in a manner neglected by Scott and necessarily precluded in the study of history alone. Slow going for the modern reader, these novels through their labored and scholarly historical accuracy won an impressively wide popular audience. However, Bulwer-Lytton, as a recent critic has noted,[11] accomplished even more than we usually recognize, having been the first to turn the historical novel to the purposes of contemporary social criticism. The analysis of social and political problems in *The Last*

11. Curtis Dahl, "History on the Hustings: Bulwer-Lytton's Historical Novels of Politics," in *From Jane Austen to Joseph Conrad*, eds. Robert C. Rathburn and Martin Steinmann, Jr. (Minneapolis, 1958), pp. 60 ff.

of the Barons, for example, was aimed at the society of Bulwer-Lytton's own day as well as that which existed during the time of the novel's setting, the period of the Wars of the Roses. Of course, the application of past historical lessons to the contemporary scene had already become a part of Victorian tradition in the writings of Carlyle and Macaulay, but Bulwer-Lytton was the first to realize its moral and political utility in terms of historical fiction.

For Ford, born in the year Bulwer-Lytton died, historical fiction was slated to become an even more forceful technique of social and political commentary. It provided him with a key to historical process itself, a key that then became the basis of those "contemporary histories" in which Ford sought to hold the mirror up to his own age. Driven like Ford by that sense of painful transition in his own society, Bulwer-Lytton had been instinctively attracted to those earlier periods suffering the dislocations of social change; and like both Ford and Scott he created characters who in themselves summed up the prevailing Zeitgeist of their day. But unlike Scott's and like Ford's, Bulwer-Lytton's protagonists come to grief because of their historical misplacement, suggesting that by mid-century Hegelian idealism was already taking on more somber hues. The majority of Bulwer-Lytton's heroes find themselves unable or unwilling to adjust to what Hegel called the altering Time Spirit. Though no Hegelian himself, Bulwer-Lytton assumed as did Carlyle the shaping influence of individual great men—Hegel's "World Individuals," the same assumption permeating Green's Short History. This is not, however, to argue any close similarity between Bulwer-Lytton's and Ford's historical works; there are deep and significant differences. The fate of Bulwer-Lytton's alien protagonists represents, as it were, a halfway point in the erosion of Hegelian idealism with historical process.

Although Bulwer-Lytton sensed that an impartial historical thrust was as apt to grind down the generous and noble while elevating the unscrupulous and mean-spirited, he agreed with Scott that the goal justified the sacrifice, that history—over the long haul—worked out for the greatest good of the greatest number. What one sees here is the last lingering vestige of Hegelian hopefulness, as yet untempered by the Franco-Prussian and Boer Wars, nor supplanted by the growing influence of Schopenhauer and Darwin. Bulwer-Lytton shared with many of his day that deeply ingrained, mid-Victorian insistence that ultimate good can come of apparent evil:

> That nothing walks with aimless feet;
> That not one life shall be destroyed,
> Or cast as rubbish to the void,
> When God hath made the pile complete.

Such a "progressive" view of historical evolution contrasts starkly with the elder Hueffer's conviction of "the revolting cruelty of Nature, which at the cost of inconceivable individual suffering creates new types only to abandon them again to the universal doom of destruction." Or Conrad's "Progress leaves its dead by the way. . . . It is a march into an undiscovered country; and in such an enterprise the victims do not count." The distance between that self-enforced mid-Victorian hopefulness and late-Victorian despair is also the distance between Ford's and Bulwer-Lytton's world views, the road down which the nineteenth century had passed from Hegelian idealism to Darwinian and Schopenhauerean gloom. And someplace along the way there died that Victorian falsification of art for purposes of moral reassurance so reprehensible to Ford, and its place taken by Zola's demand that the artist seek out and build upon some "absolute determinism for all human phenomena."

In using only Walter Scott and Bulwer-Lytton as counters against which to weigh Ford's achievement in the historical novel, one invites the danger of oversimplification. Any really complete account would have to find a place for a number of lesser figures: William Harrison Ainsworth, Robert Louis Stevenson, H. Rider Haggard, and Maurice Hewlett, to mention but a few. Ainsworth's dozen-odd historical novels represent the Gothic extreme to which the romance might be pressed in works like *Rookwood* (1834),

Windsor Castle (1843), and The Lancashire Witches (1848). As conscientiously antiquarian as Scott, Ainsworth, with his heavy strokes of local color and turgid rhetoric, detracts from the historical impression he makes. History in his work is the awkward and unwilling handmaiden to an unbridled romantic imagination. Less Gothic, if more lurid, were the sensationalistic romances of Rider Haggard. An uneasy fusion of realism and fantasy, the exotic settings of his tales covered every inch of the habitable and sometimes uninhabitable globe; and when these were exhausted in his African and Mexican novels, he retreated like Verne, Doyle, and Lytton to the earth's interior.

Though the less extravagant historical romances of Quiller-Couch (1863–1944) and Conan Doyle (1859–1930) contributed both prestige and popularity to the genre, their contribution was less technically important than that of Stevenson and his successors, who sought to introduce a deeper concern for psychological realism into the historical novel. Stevenson's psychological portrait of power politics, often and loosely called Meredithian, in Prince Otto (1885) has very nearly the dramatic force of Ford's own The Fifth Queen; and the symbolic interplay between states of mind and natural settings suggests Conrad's better short fiction. But it was in the work of two lesser contemporaries, Maurice Hewlett (1861–1923) and Neil Munro (1864–1930), that Stevenson's shrewd psychological analysis was to find its way fully into the historical romance. To Scott's love of highland lore and legend, Munro brought the historical realism of Meredith and the psychology of Stevenson. Based on the same historical events as Scott's Legend of Montrose, Munro's John Splendid (1898) shows a depth of characterization and historical accuracy far beyond Scott's work, though later novels—especially The Shoes of Fortune (1901)—tend to deteriorate into costume romance.

But it was the remorseless psychological probing of Hewlett, once praised by Ford, that readied historical fiction for twentieth-century tastes. These chronicles of "fine consciences," tapestry-like in their scenes of medieval England and their graphic descriptions of costume and architecture, suggest an indebtedness to Pre-Raphaelite paintings similar to what one finds in Ford. An early work like *The Forest Lovers* (1898) scants character psychology for the sheer excitement and atmosphere of romance, with an attempt to approximate the cadences and syntax of Malory. However, the psychological realism of his *The Life and Death of Richard Yea-and-Nay* (1900) gave to the world a violent and tempestuous Richard Coeur de Lion that Scott, for one, would never have recognized—but who dramatized that growing assumption of the essentially ferocious nature of medieval psychology. Hewlett's best work, *The Queen's Quair* (1904), created one of the finest psychological portraits the historical novel had yet seen in his character of Mary Stuart. It was unquestionably of this character that Ford was thinking when he once remarked on Hewlett's comparatively deeper concern "to keep his characters well within their historic *cadres* in the matter of psychology." [12]

That Ford believed in such "cadres" is the measure of difference between his own and Hewlett's historical perspective. For Ford, psychological types are fixed throughout history, and the forces of social selection will bring forward different types depending upon the peculiar social demands of successive periods, thereby producing those conflicts of opposed cultures that appear only in the historical fiction of Scott, Bulwer-Lytton, and himself. Though the fragmentary *Weir of Hermiston* suggests the conflict of generations, neither Stevenson, his predecessors, or his imitators belong to the main line of development reaching from Scott, through Bulwer-Lytton, down to Ford. In the work of these three men alone exists that larger sense of historical process, which in Ford's work became the basis for conflict in his novels of "contemporary history." It is in this tradition that Ford's early work through 1915 has its roots, a native English growth whose existence has been overshadowed by the

12. *Return to Yesterday*, p. 284.

more colorful clash of the decadent and counter-decadent movement. But the strain was there and it was both prolific and popular, a vigorous form belonging to neither *The Yellow Book* nor *National Observer* crowds, whose precincts Ford instinctively skirted.

Possessed of a deeper sense of history than either his Edwardian contemporaries or the French naturalists and unfearful of the "romantic taint" of medievalism, Ford, like Bulwer-Lytton before him, sought answers for the present in the problems of the past. James, Zola, and Daudet had all chosen the contemporary setting to escape the romantic unreality they wrongly associated with the historical fiction of the past. For their more restricted social determinism Ford substituted a comprehensive pattern of historical determinism, one that brought into perspective the comparative and often conflicting standards of social behavior in successive historical periods. As in Scott, these conflicts are the human and inevitable outcome of historical events themselves, but reflected immediately and dramatically in characters whose individual psychology and consequent destiny reflect larger social and historical forces behind them. Consequently the limitations in so many of Ford's protagonists, as well as the "passiveness" in Scott's is testimony to the simple fact that no man, past or present, can go beyond the determining social and historical forces of his time. Ford's achievement as a historical novelist lay in his ability to translate well-known historical figures into the believable historical-social types he had earlier described in *England and the English*, according to the pattern he had learned in his public-school reading of Green's *Short History*.

Ford's first historical novel, *The Fifth Queen*, besides embodying Ford's personal historical system, perfectly exemplifies the manner in which historical controversies had been dramatized in the earlier historical fiction of Scott and Bulwer-Lytton. The traditional setting had come to be one of turbulent transition in which a dying culture struggles for survival against a new World Spirit. By general historical consensus, the first half of the sixteenth century had long since been established as the seminal example of just such an age of transition. Ford saw in the period that final confrontation between the forces and principles of waning feudalism and those of the emergent Renaissance, and he uses it as the setting for *The Fifth Queen* and the political power struggle centering around the rise and fall of Henry VIII's fifth queen, Katherine Howard.

For a half century the Tudor crown had systematically chipped away at the remnants of baronial power in its attempt to work out the institutions of effective centralized government. By the fourth decade of the century had come the inevitable reaction to these policies. The immediate historical occasion was the simultaneous collapse of Thomas Cromwell's European diplomacy and the rising in the north against continuing monastic dissolution. With Yorkshire and Cumberland in flames, Henry was faced with the greatest crisis in his reign. In London the political struggle between the northern, Catholic reactionaries—feudal in character—and the political commoners, men of the New Learning, and Lutheran in sympathies, provided Ford with the plot, characters, and setting to implement his concept of history. The greatest personages of the age figure prominently in the foreground: Catholic insurgents like Bishop Gardiner and the Duke of Norfolk are plunged into one of those Hegelian conflicts with men of the New Learning, men like Thomas Cromwell, Archbishop Cranmer, and Nicholas Throckmorton. Although the figure of Henry VIII himself appears prominently, his political and psychological nature is left deliberately ambiguous and enigmatic for much of the novel. Into this Tudor nighttime world of political intrigue and personal betrayal comes Katherine Howard, a last bright gleam from the setting sun of feudalism. As the representative of an older world order she necessarily comes to grief in the new historical age, which takes its impulse from the renaissance Italy of Niccolo Machiavelli. As Machiavelli himself so tersely put it: "He is unfortunate whose mode of procedure is opposed to the Times." Katherine is the first of Ford's alien protagonists whose archaic ethical and psychological natures throw them into a continual moral and ideological conflict with their age and who—as recognizable historical types—are the direct outgrowth of Ford's reading of history.

The kinship between Ford's approach to historical fiction and that of his predecessor Scott is reflected in the latter's stated narrative plan for *The Monastery*, which might have served equally well for Ford's various historical works: "The general plan of the story was to conjoin two characters in that bustling and contentious age, who, thrown into situations which gave them different views on the subject of the reformation, should, with the same sincerity and purity of intention, dedicate themselves, the one to the support of the sinking fabric of the Catholic Church, the other to the establishment of the reformed doctrines."[13] This typically Waverley formula is the precise format Ford used in *The Fifth Queen;* it was, as I have shown, the one that had attached itself to the genre in the course of the nineteenth century. Behind both Ford and Scott there is this imaginative breadth of historical perspective, but there is also a deep difference. *The Monastery* deals with that same conflict between a dying feudal-Catholic culture and an insurgent Protestant one. Scott dramatizes the struggle through two purely imaginary characters: Father Eustace, a humane and compassionate priest, and a Protestant reformer, Henry Warden, no whit less admirable than his Catholic counterpart. It is almost as if the two were saying to each other: "Why be nasty about it? After all the whole business will resolve itself into the Anglo-Catholic compromise." As opposed to this Hegelian idealism, one finds in Ford's account of this religious struggle a grimmer sense of historical survival and extinction.

In showing both sides of this religious controversy Ford displayed, at least as convincingly, the piebald nature of all religious truths—without slipping into Scott's facile sentimentality. With that more hardened, post-Darwinian sense of history, Ford imagined no picturesque confrontation between noble foes—one Catholic, one

13. Walter Scott, "Introduction" to *The Monastery* (Boston and New York, 1923), p. ix.

Protestant. Instead we have two dour and hardened adversaries, the Duke of Norfolk and Thomas Cromwell, each with a measure of rightness in his cause, yet both alive to the practical exigencies of political survival. In his contrasting physical description of the two men, Ford draws most heavily on the Dürer and Holbein paintings, as he seeks to dramatize the physiognomic and psychological shift he imagined between the feudal and the renaissance worlds. The following scene lies at the heart of both his novel and his entire theory of successive psychological ages in England's history:

This Norfolk was that Earl of Surrey who had won Flodden Field. They all then esteemed him the greatest captain of his day—in the field a commander sleepless . . . in striking a Hotspur.

A dour and silent man, he was head of all the Catholics, of all the reaction of that day. But, in the long duel between himself and Cromwell he had seemed *fated* [italics mine] to be driven from pillar to post, never daring to proclaim himself openly the foe of the man he dreaded and hated. Cranmer, with his tolerant spirit, he despised. Here was an archbishop who might rack and burn for discipline's sake, and he did nothing. . . . And all these New Learning men with their powers of language, these dark bearded men with twinkling and sagacious eyes, he detested. He went clean shaven, lean and yellow-faced, with a hooked nose that seemed about to dig into his chin. It was he who said first: "It was merry in England before this New Learning came in." [14]

Passages such as this are as close as Ford ever came to making explicit the historical substructure underlying so much of his work. Only that passing reference to Norfolk's failure as "fated" betrays the deterministic system that foredooms so many in his novels. Though no protagonist, Norfolk is a characteristic representative of Ford's medieval dominant type, such as he had postulated in *England and the English* and described visually in the Holbein monograph. Ford's stock medieval figure was to recur in later novels, displaying always the same facial characteristics and disposition.

14. Ford Madox Ford, *The Fifth Queen*, in *The Bodley Head Ford Madox Ford*, ed. Graham Greene (London, 1962), p. 41. (All subsequent references will be to this edition.)

Lady Blanche d'Enguerrand of *Ladies Whose Bright Eyes* displays both Norfolk's lean, tanned countenance and martial spirit. And Squire Bettesworth in *The Portrait* (1910) is a half-serious variation of the older pre-Tudor type with both the visage and choleric disposition of Norfolk: "The flesh of his face had fallen away, so that his nose was very hooked; and his skin was gone very brown with weather and exposure." [15] Even more telling is the transformation of the hero Sorrels, a refugee in time from the twentieth century who, through a rap on the skull, finds himself transported back to the fifteenth century. Through a gradual adjustment of values, by the end of the novel he takes on the physical and psychological characteristics of Ford's medieval dominant type.

Nearly every member of the Catholic faction in *The Fifth Queen* is patterned after Ford's study of Dürer's medieval faces: lean, brown, and clean-shaven. In addition to Norfolk these medieval types include Nicholas Udal—"long, thin, brown in his doctor's gown . . . his brown, lean, shaven and humorous face . . ." (p. 12); the violent, choleric, and clean-shaven Culpepper whose eyes mirror Dürer's other worldly visionaries: that "expression of engrossed and grievous absence" (p. 50); as well as Bishop Gardiner with "the bluish tinge of his shaven jaws . . ." (p. 78).

By contrast, the Tudor Machiavellians of *The Fifth Queen* are those new dominant types Ford had described in *England and the English:* "a heavy, dark, bearded, bull-necked animal, sagacious, smiling, but with devious and twinkling eyes." [16] Foremost among this type in the novel is the character of Henry VIII, with "his enormous bulk of scarlet . . . the broad chest . . . his head hung forward as though he were about to charge the world" (p. 39). Ford's heavy emphasis on visual impressionism in creating these conflicting dominant types is worked out in part through a series of image clusters of anagogic intensity. Associated with the images of

15. Ford Madox Ford, *The Portrait* (London, 1910), p. 245.
16. Ford Madox Ford, *England and the English: An Interpretation* (New York, 1907), p. 282.

heaviness and inscrutability in the Tudor figures are those ancillary images of lightness and darkness. Images of light invariably symbolize the sunny fields of medievalism, now in threatened eclipse and unable to penetrate the darkened corridors and fog-shrouded alleyways of a Tudor London. Cromwell first appears to the reader aboard his darkened barge on the Thames at night, the only flickering light blotted out by the overshadowing bulk of his Machiavellian aide Throckmorton, whose "bearded and heavy form obscured the light." The phrase "his immense and bearded form" becomes a leit-motif of Forster-like intensity. Consequently, criticism, like that of Carol Ohmann's that Ford unnecessarily "repeats again and again a small number of adjectives such as *little, great, huge, heavy, ill,* and *goodly,*" [17] is totally beside the mark. Such detailed description was, as I have said, more than impressionistic canon; it was the indispensable adjunct to Ford's entire portrayal of various historical and psychological types.

Ford clearly intended the reader to make the obvious connection between these physical-psychological types and the historical transition taking place behind the action of the novel. As surely as with Scott, in whose tradition Ford was directly working, the contrast between the two types and their respective world views provides the major architectonic device of the book. From the opening to the closing scene of *The Fifth Queen* and through three successive levels of Tudor society, Ford traces the conflict of his warring Time Spirits. The opening scene of the novel is appropriately set in Austin Friars, a hotbed of religious and political controversy in its day. Standing before the print shop of John Badge is Nicholas Udal. The scene within the shop dramatizes Ford's historical process operative at the lowest level of Tudor society. Old Badge, the father, a recusant Catholic two generations old with "shaven chin," taunts his dour Lutheran son, "square, dark, with . . . his black beard and . . . heavy brows" (p. 14), as they argue over Cromwell's antipapal

17. Carol Ohmann, *Ford Madox Ford* (Middletown, Conn., 1964), p. 25.

policies. Here begin those symbolic physiognomies first described by Ford in his Holbein monograph and now made a part of the historic-symbolic system of the early novels. In this same scene Ford introduces the Machiavellian atmosphere of Tudor politics with the first direct reference to Thomas Cromwell, the embodiment of the Italian's political philosophy. Udal advises an ambitious young courtier that "for instruction in the books of the Sieur Macchiavelli [sic] let young Poins go to a man who had studied them word by word—to the Lord Privy Seal, Thomas Cromwell" (p. 23). The association of Cromwellian policy with Machiavelli's political theory had become a truism among English historians long before Ford wrote, but nowhere more strongly than in Green's Short History, from which Ford borrowed reported comments of Henry's most able adviser.

After a scene of public riot in which Lutherans battle Catholics in the precincts of the palace itself, Cromwell and Norfolk are summoned before Henry to explain the internecine brawls of their followers. Ford has broadened his portrait of an England racked by religious schism from Austin Friars, through the streets of London, to the royal court itself. In achieving this cross-section of Tudor London, Ford moves his narrative through three self-enclosed and concentric circles of action. This strongly centripetal structure in the novel is essentially that of Scott's Kenilworth and, especially, Bulwer-Lytton's The Last of the Barons; and, like Scott's The Monastery, it uses paired characters to suggest the renaissance-medieval controversy. Ford's scenes, however, follow one another with a swiftness equal to those of Conrad's Chance, which also makes use of the centripetal structure. The dully mechanistic structure of The Fifth Queen represents a congenital weakness that was to plague Ford throughout his early works. It was the negative aspect of the legacy he inherited from Scott and the entire tradition of the historical novel, and one he was long in overcoming.

As the narrative focus of The Fifth Queen moves toward dead center, the upper levels of Tudor society, each successive concentric circle has its own chief participant, as well as its own minor characters; and the point of view in each section shifts between these groups, creating that sense of depth and breadth unusual to the historical novel. The movement of action *within* these circles, though Ford uses both vertical and horizontal time, is purely causal; but *between* the circles of action themselves there is no sense of connection or logical continuity—no narrative or structural device to hold together these centripetal spheres of action, only that pervasive sense of historical flux everywhere.

The essence of the novel is that continual contrast of character and action, of old versus new; and yet its principal character, Katherine Howard, hangs poised in isolation between the two groups. Ford's first alien protagonist—one of those antiquated survivors of a bygone era—Katherine is at constant loggerheads with the new World Spirit. For all of Ford's historical misfits, an adjustment can always be made; but adjustment, said Ford, was not the stuff of "romance"—that was "principle, [which] is wrongheadedness wrought up to the sublime pitch. . . ." The key to survival within Ford's system of historical evolution was adaption, and Katherine, like the greatest of Ford's protagonists, chooses not to adapt. She has as little in common with her Catholic kinsman Norfolk, who exemplifies that "predatory instinct for survival" a recent historian noted of all the Howards,[18] as she does with her Protestant antagonist Cromwell. An anachronism of religious and moral certitude in the new age of ethical relativism, she listens with dumb incomprehension to the Machiavellian Throckmorton's dismissal of her medieval world order where an absolute good confronted absolute evil: "Why, dear heart . . . those were the days of a black or white world; now we are all grey or piebald" (p. 171). To this representative of the new dominant type, Katherine's refusal to dabble in the conspiratorial waters of Tudor politics, to meet caprice with caprice seems quixotic and self-destructive. It is, as he tells her, "a folly to

18. Lacey Baldwin Smith, *A Tudor Tragedy: The Life and Times of Catherine Howard* (New York, 1961), p. 9.

be too proud to fight the world with the world's weapons" (p. 154). At this point in the novel Throckmorton has not yet grasped that this is not Katherine's world, nor that her weapons and instincts are of another time and place. Naive and stiff-necked as she is, Katherine's fealty to an older ethical norm, like Tietjens' and Ashburnham's after her, is Ford's ironic device for suggesting the loss of probity and honor with the birth of the Renaissance, a continuing deterioration he was to trace down to modern times.

Ford's character of Katherine is nevertheless a far cry from the sentimental reconstruction of her character one finds in Miss Strickland's historical account, which pictures her as a confused and wide-eyed girl-queen, victimized by the ruthless masculinity of the Tudor world and "led like a sheep to the slaughter." As an embodiment of Ford's medieval type, she is physically powerful ("I am stronger than most men" [p. 118]) and retains the medievalist's penchant for directness and violence. Capable, in a moment of anger, of beating a prostrate servant with the fire tongs, her impulsive temper consistently sets her off from those around her. It is she who puts into words what her more cautious and politic kinsman most longs for in his secret soul: Cromwell's head on a salver. Contemptuous of Machiavellian intrigue, its habit of "moving in the dark, listening at pierced walls, swearing of false treasons," Katherine constitutes Ford's conception of the medieval personality—paradoxically capable of both intense religiosity and direct violence. In a deeply symbolic action during a crucial scene near the close of *The Fifth Queen*, she defends herself by plunging her crucifix, its point sharpened to that of a poinard, into her antagonist's shoulder. Taine, who had criticized Scott's romantic suppression of medieval violence, its "plain spoken words, licentious sensuality, bestial ferocity," [19] would have applauded Ford's rendering of the medieval personality. Certainly no Scott heroine ever came on the scene like

---

19. Hippolyte A. Taine, *History of English Literature*, trans. H. Van Laun (New York, 1965), III, 436.

Ford's Katherine Howard, or Lady Dionissia, who unhorses her male adversary, the Knight of Coucy, in *Ladies Whose Bright Eyes*. Of the two dozen odd characters in the book only Katherine Howard and her choleric cousin-suitor Culpepper represent Ford's pure medieval types. Innocents abroad in a world they never made, theirs is a deterministic tragedy of historical misplacement, their presence on the Tudor scene hardly more incongruous than Dickens' Megalosaurus dragging its serpentine length up Holborn Hill on the opening page of *Bleak House*. Other Catholic noblemen and churchmen Ford depicts as masters at hounds and hares. Running now with the one, now with the other, they are simply the praying wing of the Tudor Machiavellians, refusing to understand—as Katherine does—that papal re-establishment without restitution is to make a political mockery of papal authority. They jockey for position under any dispensation; she stands upright in "that sea of error," her eyes fixed on God's kingdom. It is, in fact, solely through his use of eye imagery that Ford distinguishes between pure medieval types, like Katherine and Culpepper, and those political trimmers who hasten to make their adjustments to the new world order. Though possessing the physiology and physiognomy of Dürer's portraits, these trimmers lack one telltale feature of the thoroughgoing medieval type: the dreaming eyes of the religious idealist. It was Dürer, painting during what Ford called the "twilight of the gods," who captured in the eyes of his medieval subjects that intensity of religious vision. "In his portraits the eyes dream, accept or believe in the things they see." [20] Borrowing from Ruskin's assumption of the eye as the gateway to the soul, Ford noted the change in the eyes of Holbein's renaissance subjects. "The eyes in Holbein's portraits . . . are half closed, skeptical, challenging and disbelieving." [21] Consequently the eye itself becomes a symbolic index of historical orientation. Those of the Tudor figures "nar-

20. Ford Madox Ford, *Hans Holbein the Younger: A Critical Monograph* (Chicago and New York, 1914), p. 13.
21. *Ibid.*

row," "dart," or "lower" by turns. The eyes of Cromwell himself are described as "dangerous," those of his secretary Viridius "furtive," the King's "crafty." By contrast, the medieval figures possess eyes "wide open . . . amazed," like those of Dürer's mystics, "gazing at nothing."

Repeatedly and explicitly Ford associates medieval religious idealism with his protagonist Katherine's openness of countenance: "Papistry and a loyal love for the Old Faith seemed to be as strong in her candid eyes as it was implicit in her name" (p. 76). On the other hand, while men like Udal, Gardiner, and Norfolk obviously figure as medieval physical and physiognomic types, their eyes betray them for the political weathercocks they are—men trying desperately to adjust to the altered Time Spirit. Their faces appear to Cromwell in a moment of reverie: "The very faces of his enemies seemed visible to him. He saw Gardiner, of Winchester, with his snake's eyes under the flat cap, and the Duke of Norfolk with his eyes malignant in a long, yellow face." (p. 31) The eyes of Katherine, by contrast, are always those of the dreamer, the visionary, who even in moments of great personal danger is described with eyes fixed afar, smiling, beatific, seeing Dürer's "mystical doubles" behind all phenomenal objects, sights beyond the ken of the Tudor Machiavellians, those human symbols for the Protestant growth of skeptical pragmatism. In her myopic idealism she stumbles toward the block in the unfamiliar moral terrain of their later age.

Sir Thomas Culpepper, the only other pure medieval type, and like Katherine a child of the north, exists primarily as an extension of Katherine's own feudal proclivities toward violence. Volatile by temperament, fanatical in his devotion to Katherine, he barely rises above a humor character drawn from medieval drama. The easy dupe of Ford's Machiavellians, he is the sole male representative of that turbulent medieval world. Choleric in speech and action, he seems at best a clownish Quentin Durward, unable to find his bearings amidst the conspiratorial jungle of Tudor politics. Although he never rises above a tissue-thin caricature of that chivalric-feudal ideal represented by Katherine, he does represent a less complex example of Ford's medieval dominant type. In dramatizing his historical thesis of conflict and change, Ford had recourse to three groupings of characters in *The Fifth Queen:* the declining and outmaneuvered medieval types, the new Tudor men of policy, and in between the political trimmers, short on principles, but long on survival instinct, a trait for which the Howards were proverbial. Dancing to the unfamiliar strains of the Tudor fandango, threading their uneasy course between past and present, they are Ford's fictional embodiment of the Hegelian World Spirit, seeking that synthesis of the *via media,* a historical movement Ford was to suggest even more strongly in *The "Half-Moon,"* written the following year. In his later novels Ford relied increasingly upon an alien ethical persona by which he might implicitly criticize the contemporary scene. The genesis of the technique lies in the type of psychological oppositions he creates in the Tudor trilogy and the historical syntheses that grow out of these dramatic oppositions. Katherine, intelligent and attractive as Ford makes her, might well have turned England and Henry back into the Catholic fold, had Cromwell and Protestantism been her sole adversaries, but they were not. It is the very tenor of the times, the historical *Zeitgeist,* against which Katherine struggles. Her absolutist mentality grasps too late the dominant psychological temper of the new years: "It was not . . . any more a world of black and white that she saw, but a world of men who did one thing in order that something very different might happen a long time afterwards" (p. 186). Such is the nature of that self-knowledge that Ford once noted "always comes too late."

The tragedy of Katherine Howard, caught up and destroyed within Ford's deterministic world machine, reflects in part his legacy from French Naturalism. From that elaborate conceptual grid he imposed upon English history, he constructed protagonists who represent that absolute psychological determinism that Zola, and after him Flaubert and de Maupassant, called for. Repeatedly in

Ford's early novels, his behind-the-scenes historical mythos provided him with a solution to what he saw as the novelist's most
pressing problem: "The problem of the author is to make his then
action the only action that character could have taken. It must be
inevitable, because of his character, because of his ancestry . . . or
on account of the gradual coming together of the thousand small
circumstances by which Destiny, who is inscrutable and august, will
push us into one certain predicament." [22] Although Zola was merely
reflecting that current vogue within the arts for an alliance with the
exactitude of scientific method, Ford's approach represents a fusion
of historical theory and biological evolutionism, darkened by the *fin
de siècle* gloom of Schopenhauerean determinism, inherited from his
father. The immediate sources of the cultural and psychological
conflicts underlying the dramatic structure of *The Fifth Queen* are
found in the final book of *England and the English;* but behind that
chapter lies the influence of J. R. Green's *A Short History of the
English People*, and still further back those widely but vaguely
inherited notions of early nineteenth-century historical theorists like
Hegel, Carlyle, Buckle, and Froude.

The most distinctive break with traditional history writing was
Green's rejection of traditional historical divisions into reigns or
dynasties. Instead he arranged them according to their dominant
character or mood, the concepts and ideals that typified them, as
well as the individuals who embodied them—exactly as Ford would
do three decades later in *England and the English*. Subsequently the
period of the New Learning, easily the finest in the book, Green
describes as "the history of a single man," Thomas Cromwell, to
whom he devotes some twenty pages. And yet neither Green, nor
Ford, who followed him, fully accepted the "Great Man" theory of
history espoused by Carlyle and Froude. Green more resembles
Renan, who argues the balance of collective achievement with that
of individual achievement, while Ford's theory suggests Buckle's
unfinished *History of Civilization in England* (1857–1861), with its

22. Ford, *Joseph Conrad*, p. 219.

emphasis upon the impersonal and deterministic forces behind historical movement. But the proliferation of historical theories during the nineteenth century makes such conjecture a hey, nonny-nonny game, except where direct influence can be shown, as with Ford and Green. What Ford unquestionably took from Green was the historian's glimpse of the entire evolutionary sweep of English history, a presentation given immediacy by what one intellectual historian described as a "drama in the contrast of social types." [23]

Ford's high regard for Cromwell's achievement simply echoes Green's own judgment. It was a conviction Ford repeated throughout his life, seeing in Cromwell, as he did, an ordered and definite purpose, free of the muddle and drift of subsequent English statecraft—that continual fluctuation between the libertarian chaos of Gladstone and the mindless reactionism of the Salisbury government. This conviction he voiced not only in *England and the English*, but in the *English Review*, *The Critical Attitude*, even in the "historical vignettes" he later wrote for *Outlook*. Consequently in the opening chapter of *The Critical Attitude*, when scoring the modern Britisher's lack of critical intelligence, the wavering "between statecraft and mercy," Ford summons up the remembrance of Cromwell's consistent and inexorable purpose so well suited to an earlier age of transition and strife. It was the same characteristic Green had discerned in the Tudor statesmen: "He is, in fact, the first English minister in whom we can trace through the whole period of his rule the steady working out of a great and definite purpose. His purpose was to raise the King to absolute authority on the ruins of every rival power within the realm." [24] And so it is that Ford's Cromwell speaks of his personal mission in *The Fifth Queen*, in one of the novel's typically structured interior monologues:

He would be perpetually beside the throne, there would be no distraction to maintain a foothold. He would be there by right; he would be able to give all his mind to the directing of this world that he despised for its

23. Emery Neff, *The Poetry of History* (New York, 1947), p. 185.
24. John Richard Green, *A Short History of the English People* (London, 1875), p. 328.

baseness, its jealousies, its insane brawls, its aimless selfishness, and its blind furies. Then there should be no more war, as there should be no more revolts. There should be no more jealousies; for kingcraft, solid, austere, practical and inspired, should keep down all the peoples, all the priests, and all the nobles of the world. [p. 30]

Though less lyric in his appraisal of Cromwell than Froude had been, Green recognized in this lowborn son of a brewer the man who—in Ford's own phrase—had "welded England into one formidable whole." [25]

Ruthless and cruel as it had been, Ford discerned in Cromwell's ministry a saving interlude of "realism" between two ages of political "romanticism," the feudal and the Puritan. With the death of feudal idealism, and after the Cromwellian interlude, came Puritanism with its confusion of church and state, which in Ford's mind was foredoomed to collapse into the invertebrate and disssident political mobocracy—once its religious impulse died—of Ford's own day. The medieval scene, with its strict religious and sociopolitical structuring, had escaped this, but a Puritan England had no such safeguard and had since Cromwell's time wavered indecisively between "statecraft and mercy." Hence comes that sometimes confusing contradiction between Ford's genuine admiration for feudalism and his no less genuine affection for the political figure who brought its house crashing down about its ears. Quasi-Catholic, feudalist, and Tory that he was, Ford sensed that the subsequent Puritan age lacked both the sustaining structural and spiritual integrity of Catholicism and the political realism of the Tudor Machiavels.

From Green's text as well Ford gained his first insight into the Machiavellian nature both of Cromwell and of the age whose principles he embodied. Green had argued that Cromwell's success stemmed from the absolute identification of his personal aims with those of the New Learning itself. [26] And Green's *Short History* had concluded that only with the appearance of Cromwell did the

25. *England and the English*, p. 283.
26. *Short History*, p. 345.

Machiavellian spirit enter into sixteenth-century English politics:
"Not only in the rapidity and ruthlessness of his designs, but in their
larger scope, their clearer purpose, and their admirable combination,
the Italian state-craft entered with Cromwell into politics." [27] Trans-
lated into Ford's condensed version of historical evolution and of
those successive psychological ages, Cromwell, in *England and the
English*, is pictured as a new "splendid and efficient dominant type,"
a product of that mysterious social selectivity that has always been
England's salvation: "Italy which produced Macchiavelli [*sic*],
failed utterly to profit by him. England, on the other hand . . .
profited exceedingly. . . . It *did* produce from its depths, from
amidst its bewildering cross currents of mingled races, *the* great man
of its age; and, along with him, it produced a number of men similar
in type. . . . The man, of course, was Thomas Cromwell. . . ." [28]

One of Green's most significant contributions to the art of historical writing was to introduce, wherever possible, telling glimpses or
quotations from the lives of his historical personages. The dramatic
effectiveness of the technique was not lost on the young Ford, who
never forgot Green's emphasis upon the close connection between
the Florentine thinker and his English disciple: "His statesmanship
was closely modelled on the ideal of the Florentine thinker whose
book was constantly in his hand. Even as a servant of Wolsey he
startled the future Cardinal, Reginald Pole, by bidding him take for
his manual in politics the 'Prince' of Machiavelli." [29] Ford simply
"lifted" this historical scene from Green, altered it by substituting a
minor figure for Pole, and made it a crucial scene in the second
novel of the trilogy. This is Cromwell, laying before his lieutenant
Lascalles the secret of his own success: " 'Read well in this,' he said,
'where much I have read. You shall see in it mine own annotations.
This is *Il Principe* of Machiavelli; there is none other book like it in
the world. Study of it well: read it upon your walks. I am a simple

27. *Ibid.*, p. 328.
28. *England and the English*, pp. 282–83.
29. *Short History*, p. 328.

man, yet it hath made me.' " (*Privy Seal*, p. 386) In summary, the seminal influence of Green's *Short History* upon Ford's concept of history, as that conception is expressed in both his fiction and nonfiction, is clearly demonstrable in four major areas: first, in the general and over-all movement of history itself, that gradual evolution of the English temper, reflected in an altering intellectual climate of dominant ideas, a prevailing *Zeitgeist* that expresses itself through a contrast of social types. Secondly, there is the high priority given to this specific period, a crucial era of transition between the medieval and modern world. Thirdly, Ford, like Green, singles out Thomas Cromwell, Lord Privy Seal, as the man most characteristic of the new Italianate political influence and the man best suited by temperament to successfully apply those doctrines to the English scene. And, finally, Green's attempt to dramatize British history visually and audibly provided Ford with some of his most powerful individual scenes. Ford may possibly have confirmed his opinion of Cromwell and the Tudor age in readings subsequent to Green's *A Short History of the English People*, though his references to his own scholarship are both ambiguous and self-contradictory. What is unambiguous and indisputable is that at the moment of articulating his historical thesis, it was the remembrance of Green's account that came into his mind and to which he specifically refers as he does to no other historian.

Despite Ford's deep indebtedness to past chronicle, history simply provided the spur to Ford's imagination rather than a literal basis on which his tales were to be built. Ford's contempt for academic historians, those "learned Puffendorfiuses" as he called them, shaped a certain predilection for revisionist history—whether on the historical question of Katherine's guilt, or that apocryphal anecdote he had from an American lady about Marshal Ney having escaped to the United States after Waterloo, where he lived out the remainder of his life in disguise someplace in New Orleans. Ford seldom felt any compunction about altering the facts of history in favor of some larger, grander scheme of historical significance. He was, after all, an impressionist, the self-professed heir of the French naturalist, who had argued, as did Maupassant, that the artist "must necessarily manipulate events."[30] And as a historical novelist writing when solipsistic history was in its heyday, Ford continually distinguished between the artist who gifts the reader with a sense of history and those "veracity mad" scientific historians like Hume whose "mole-work lucubrations" give us the exact detail of the leaf while riding blindly past the forest. Subsequently Ford's contempt for "the serious—and so portentous!—Chronicler" is scattered throughout his writings from *The Critical Attitude* (1911), *Between St. Dennis and St. George* (1915), his essay "On Impressionism" in *Poetry and Drama* (June 2, 1914) down through *Provence* (1935), but is perhaps most trenchantly set forth in his "Dedication" to *A Little Less Than Gods*, a novel set loosely against a background of Napoleonic conflict: "For I bet that your sense—not your details—of mediaeval life came to you from Scott and your mental colouration of seventeenth-century France from *The Three Musketeers*, and that, fill in your details afterwards how you may, your sense and your mental colouration are truer to the real right thing in history than all the mole-work lucubrations of the most learned of contemporary Puffendorfiuses. Or Should I write Puffendorfii?"[31]

Aside from his distrust of these "Puffendorfii," there are obvious thematic reasons for the historical alterations Ford makes in the Tudor trilogy, reasons integrally related to his concept of historical process. Early Ford criticism passed by these alterations in silence; neither Wiley nor Cassell says anything of them, nor for that matter do the later studies by MacShane and Lid. Meixner limits his discussion to Ford's apparent whitewash of Katherine's character. By the end of the novel, Meixner argues, she dwindles "into a stock sentimental heroine" whose structural function is to point up the basic

30. Guy de Maupassant, *Pierre et Jean*, in *The Works of Guy de Maupassant* (New York, 1909), VIII, 5.
31. Ford Madox Ford, "Dedication" to *A Little Less Than Gods* (New York, 1928), p. ix.

conflict of the novel, the struggle between "the rival claims of God and Caesar,"[32] which is the way Meixner reads what is actually the conflict between the medieval and Renaissance spirits. Ohmann accepts Meixner's position, arguing that though Ford altered Katherine's character "if not from history at least from the consensus of historical opinion,"[33] he failed to make her a consistent character, and was guilty of turning her into a picture of hunted virtue, "mature and steadfast—patient with others' impatience, kind in the face of cruelty."[34] This would indeed be a serious charge if it were true, but it is only partially the case, as a glance at the closing book of the trilogy reveals. Ford's handling of Katherine's character does undergo a transformation, but not simply through carelessness. It was a deliberate attempt to correct what he realized was a debilitating weakness in her character throughout *The Fifth Queen*.

There is far less sweetness and light in Katherine's transformation than Meixner and Ohmann infer. Her manner with her uncle, Norfolk, is sharp and admonitory beyond anything in the earlier novels. She dismisses Udal, her one-time tutor and confidant, to lifelong celibacy, and refuses to compromise her unbending religiosity to save a friend from the onus of bearing a bastard. And with Henry, who still loves her, she is bitter and uncompromising. There is little suggestion here of either undue patience or kindness. Actually there is a firming up of her character, a final return to the rigidity of outlook discernible in the first novel, an inflexibility tinged with the bitter melancholy of exhausted hope as she realizes her inadequacy before this new world. In order to maintain that essential opposition of past and present, which is the true center of the book, Katherine had to remain the medieval religious idealist— impatient, if not impervious, to compromise—one finds in the opening and closing books, a woman whose devout Catholicism in no way contradicts her strongly sensual and stiff-necked nature. The

32. John A. Meixner, *Ford Madox Ford's Novels* (Minneapolis, 1962), p. 47.
33. Ohmann, *Ford Madox Ford*, p. 26.
34. *Ibid.*, p. 28.

difficulty sensed in Katherine's character by Meixner and Ohmann is really owing to Ford's failure to successfully resolve the problem of fusing convincingly a historical type with a character of flesh and blood—of making the former understandable and implicit in the latter. Ford's initial alteration of Katherine's character, as well as his shifting presentation in *Privy Seal*, was dictated by his insistence upon presenting her as the embodiment of the medieval ideal and yet keeping her human and individualized at the same time.

The situation in which Katherine Howard finds herself, as Ford describes it in the novel, is historically accurate. The political maneuvering in the early summer of 1540 was the logical outgrowth of three different but interrelated crises in religion, politics, and court personalities. Into this hornet's nest of intrigue Katherine was drawn from the moment of her entrance into the court. The forces of feudal reactionism in religion and politics stood eyeball to eyeball with the advocates of all clerical and temporal revolution. But the Katherine of renaissance report was hardly Ford's prototype of all that was admirable in the feudal spirit. In actual fact she seems to have been a vain, petty, and unscrupulous young woman, incapable of inspiring love or loyalty in anyone other than the aging, unpredictable Henry, who sought to recover his lost youth in her undeniable beauty and passion. Although many, including very nearly the entire Howard clan, fell from favor at her disgrace, it was through innocent association rather than loyalty to her person that they were punished by attainder. That she was unable to command the loyalty of a single follower tells more heavily against her character than the official court records with their charges of lewdness, abandon, and concupiscence.

Ford, by contrast, creates a Katherine high-souled and proud, contemptuous of compromise, as he points up that essential conflict between her medieval idealism and the political pragmatism of the Tudor world. Such alterations as exist in her character stem from Ford's concern to remain true to the concept of history that he had learned from Green and that formed the basis of his own personal scheme of historical process and conflict. And yet there remains the slimmest possibility that Katherine was less depraved than the court records testify. Ford had, in fact, put his finger on the weakest point in history's case against Katherine: the questionable reliability of the government reports, elicited by torture and hurried forward by the political struggle going on within the court. In sum total, the only uncontroverted fact established by her interrogators was that Katherine was not a virgin at the time of her marriage to Henry. Inasmuch as she had admitted the king himself to her favors at least three months earlier, she hardly could have been! In the midst of such uncertainty Ford chose to leave the entire matter of her alleged adultery an open question to the end of the book; Katherine's own allusions to her early life are always chary and enigmatic. The Machiavellian atmosphere of the entire novel warns the reader to expect the falsification of the court records and to realize that Katherine's black name in history was the result of Tudor political expediency. It is doubtful that Katherine's own contemporaries had any clearer insight into the truth of the matter. At any rate, Ford's entire handling of historical fact falls within the precincts of Aristotelian "probability," and chastity after all was no requisite for Ford's medieval dominant type.

Ford's equation of the medieval world with the golden age of Rome did, however, make it necessary to alter much about Katherine's intelligence and education. To be a proper archetype of his medieval figure it was necessary to gift her with more intellectual equipment than her historical counterpart. Yet this is less true of Katherine's character in the first novel of the trilogy than it is in the later ones. Although Katherine's character clearly indicates her unlikeness to those around her, her alien temperament has no *raison d'être* in *The Fifth Queen*. What she is *not* is painfully, dramatically clear; but what she *is*, from whence she has come, and what the origin of her strangely vestigial nature are not made clear in the first novel of the trilogy. There is, in short, no "objective correlative" to make her alien actions and sentiments explicable. Between Ford's impressionistic restraint and his *sub rosa* historical system, he often demands more from the reader's deductions than he can fairly expect. His unconscious realization of this leads to those frequent breakdowns near the end of Ford's novel where one character is brought forward to explain to another, and to the reader, the background reasons why things should have worked out in such a fashion.

Sensing the inadequacy of his protagonist's unworldliness, of her entire motivation, Ford set out to remedy the deficiency in *Privy Seal*, the second novel of the series, by sketching in new expository material on Katherine's early childhood, which helps explain the woman before us. In the first novel Ford had largely ignored the source of Katherine's unworldliness, content to rely on that personal myth of successive dominant psychological types, unfortunately beyond the reader's horizon. In *Privy Seal*, published the year following, Ford returns to Katherine's youth, interpolating certain background material, which should more logically have appeared in the first book. Her early education, under the tutorship of Magister Udal, had been a very cloistered one—all of her precepts, all of her ethical standards have come not from the present age but from the literature of the Golden Age of Rome, from the writings of Seneca, Plutarch, and Tacitus, the darlings of the medieval schoolmen. Actually the reading Ford attributes to the youthful Katherine was that laid out for the education of Mary and her half-sister Elizabeth.

When Katherine first appears in the second novel she is shown busily arming herself with little sententious truisms culled from these ancient writers; these in hand she is about to confront Cromwell, the cynical, pragmatic student of a later Italy: "And she had read and learned by heart passages from Plutarch, from Tacitus, from Diodorus Siculus, from Seneca and from Tully, each one inculcating how salutary a thing in man was the love of justice. Therefore she felt herself well prepared to try a fall with the chief enemy of her faith, and awaited with impatience his summons to speak with him." (*Privy Seal*, p. 278) Although Katherine's idealism is as inadequate for her situation here as it was in *The Fifth Queen*, it has at least the virtue of a concrete source; Ford has given her proud and stiff-necked principles a biographical explanation they lacked in the first novel; but in doing so he had to fly in the face of historical fact. In creating a Katherine convincing in herself, yet representative of his preconceived medieval dominant type, Ford took his greatest liberties with historical fact, by making of his protagonist a deeply learned woman.

In point of fact, the historical Katherine had little by way of formal education. She had, as one historian has said, "few intellectual accomplishments, and it was considered unnecessary that she should." [35] Certainly she was not the third-ranking Latinist in the realm as Ford portrays her; and the real Katherine's labored love scrawls to Thomas Culpepper testify to her considerable difficulties with English itself. Nor is there any evidence to show that Nicholas Udal ever came into contact with Katherine—early or late in her career. Briefly Udal did attract the attention of Katherine Parr, but this was long after Katherine Howard had gone to the block and after Udal's own dismissal from Eton—not for lechery, as Ford suggests, but for certain "unnatural" behavior while in residence. And the secret marriage, attributed by Ford to Udal, was really Cranmer's and was continually held over that archbishop's head by Cromwell. But the major alterations were confined to Katherine's character and to her relationships with her "cousin" Culpepper. And here Ford followed, surprisingly, the least reliable histories of the period. Either from Strickland's *Lives of the Queens of England*, the old *Spanish Chronicle of Henry VIII*, or some equally inaccurate account Ford picked up the apochryphal tale of Katherine and Culpepper having been infants together in the same nursery. Ford was beyond such crude appeal to Victorian sentimentality, with its conditioned compassion for the "hapless child" seduced by "a low

35. Smith, *A Tudor Tragedy*, p. 48.

born villain" (Strickland). But a depraved Katherine in no way fitted Ford's conception of the medieval idealist, so he accepted the revisionist fictions of the Victorians for thematic reasons.

In all of his historical alterations Ford's primary concern was to create a Katherine Howard who embodied the temperament and virtues he, rightly or wrongly, associated with feudal England. And to do this he had to alter perceptibly Katherine's character as history had recorded it. This is not to argue that Ford was engaged in an uncritical historical whitewash simply to document his historical thesis, for he hardly expected his protagonist to excite the reader's unqualified respect any more than she did his; this was simply his objective judgment upon history and its random use of human nature. Within its amoral onward rush the dangers that threaten an idealist like Katherine are little different from those that beset cynical realists like Cromwell: both are susceptible to the temptation of pride, the rise and fall of historical cycle, as Ford once noted: "The fall of the idealist seems to be greater than the fall of a cynic, because he maintains that the world is perfectible. Yet, actually, idealist and cynic are of one flesh, and the temptation that brings down the one is none the less great for the other." [36] Katherine, the medieval idealist, is nevertheless a moving, even tragic figure, exhibiting all those usual symptoms of *hubris*. What brings about her downfall is that prideful refusal to accommodate herself to an alien cultural milieu, that stubborn refusal to admit—until too late—the antiquity of her own principles. Refusing the aid of her Machiavellian admirer, Throckmorton, who vainly reminds her that "the days of the Crusades be over," she speaks for a dying feudal aristocracy: "You be a child of the new Italians and I a disciple of the older holders of that land . . ." (*Privy Seal*, p. 349). Ford was to rely increasingly upon this type of alien ethical persona by which he might throw into starker relief a given historical scene, where loss of

36. *England and the English*, p. 352.

fixed principle and historical perspective made self-analysis impossible. The genesis of this technique lies in the type of historical oppositions one finds in the Tudor trilogy.

The self-knowledge and destruction that come to Katherine Howard come as well to her modern counterparts in the later novels, those strangely vestigial figures who belong to an age other than that in which sheer accident of birth places them. At worst these protagonists are meddlers in the affairs of an age they totally misunderstand; at best, quasi-tragic figures foredoomed to failure within the framework of Ford's historical myth. Either way their very failure becomes an indictment of the modern spirit.

Unsuccessful in *The Inheritors* at dramatizing the spectacle of cultural disintegration he perceived behind England's imperialistic adventuring, Ford discovered in the settled conflicts of earlier English history that method of isolating a protagonist from his temporal milieu. In formulating his personal and solipsistic theory of history, he learned gradually and with varying degrees of success to portray implicitly the ruthless and inexorable movement of history which grinds down men of principle and conviction. From the crude fantasy of an evolutionary romance like *The Inheritors*, with its man of honor helpless against soulless schemers from another dimension, Ford fabricated the Hegel-like concept of historical movement that gave him a framework within which to work. And though it was the historical past that first provided him with his peculiar and recurrent protagonist, one of time's dispossessed, his novels of contemporary society bear as well the indelible imprint of that same overriding world order.

# 4. Between Two Worlds

During five successive years, from 1906 to 1910, Ford was at work writing a series of historical novels that, when completed, would trace the growth of the "English Spirit" down to the threshold of Edwardian England. A year later came the strange attempt to contrast immediately the relative values of medievalism with those of the twentieth century in *Ladies Whose Bright Eyes*. Artistically the book was a failure, but it indicates the direction Ford was pursuing. Alongside his output of historical fiction, two novels appeared that were set in the twentieth century, both of which have as their central characters variations upon the alien protagonist figure, which continues to occupy a central position in the historical novels.

The year following the conclusion of the three Tudor novels (1909) saw the publication of *The "Half-Moon,"* an account of Henry Hudson's voyage to the New World. The novel describes the next phase in the psychological development of the English people against the background of that continuing breakdown in the old religious and economic order. In the preface to the novel Ford professes, somewhat unconvincingly, a deep and abiding interest in the psychological temper that marks Hudson's age, which in his mind marked the final submergence of the medieval world order: "Fortunately for me the psychology of the Old World in the days of Hudson has always been very fascinating to me. It is, as you know, the subject to which I have more than anything devoted my attention: for at that date the Dark Ages were finally breaking up."[1] The *"Half-Moon"* shows Ford's World Spirit again on the move, the old dominant type of the Tudor period now faced in its turn with a changing world scene where its once fortuitous traits are no longer those required of the times; and its figure is about to be supplanted by yet another ascendant type. The central character, Edward Colman, Hudson's second-in-command, occupies a position within the novel analogous to Katherine Howard's in the Tudor trilogy, and represents Ford's second experiment with the alien protagonist, that modulated hero upon which he was also at work in his novels of the contemporary world.

Ford's entire historical system, as we have seen, had been thought out as early as 1907 and set down in the third and final section of *England and the English*, entitled "The Spirit of the People." The major characteristic of the system is that abhorrence of stasis, so that even before the Middle Ages has disappeared, the World Individuals who replaced that age, the shrewd and unscrupulous Tudor men of policy, were themselves beginning to be pressed by still a new figure, one that embodies a subsequent Time Spirit. Even as the old dominant types disappear, so too do the temperament, the physiognomies, and the philosophical assumptions they exemplified: "This splendid and efficient dominant type had, of course, its apogee, its crest of the wave and its decline. It fell a little low with the second of the Stuart kings and, as far as international expression was concerned, its place was taken by the new, Puritan type."[2]

1. Ford Madox Ford, "Introduction" to *The "Half-Moon": A Romance of the Old World and the New* (London, 1909), p. vi. (All future references will be to this edition.)

2. Ford Madox Ford, *England and the English: An Interpretation* (New York, 1907), p. 283.

It was Ford's Puritan figure who was to become the dominant type down to the Edwardian period, a type with its own particular physiognomy, temperament, and ruling passion, "a dominant type that was fair-haired; ingenuous perhaps, unimaginative perhaps, but 'sentimental.' " [3] England's continuing rise to a position of prominence in world affairs comes because once again it is able to dip down into its heterogeneous racial stock and come up with the type best fitted to excel in the rising age. This was the Dutch-German Protestant blood strain recently driven from the Low Countries under the harrying of the Duke of Alva. These were the low country refugees who, according to Ford, had settled largely in the area of the Cinque Ports, a locale upon which he had done considerable research and written one historical and descriptive book. On the background of the Cinque Ports population, Ford later wrote in *England and the English:* "You have only to go back a generation or so to find its introduction into England. In Ben Jonson's day the Puritan was still being laughed at for a Low Country sniffler in black; within a generation the strain was ruling in England." [4]

Discernible in the long process of Ford's cyclicalism is history's continuing momentum toward a state of being most simply described as "efficiency," a term always used with opprobrium by Ford and associated in his mind with the modern Teutonic ideal. The entire historical process was hurried forward by a rigorous process of social selection based on a Darwinian indifference to humanistic values. Thus though the Puritan period reflected a movement toward the idea of action based on "principle," it was only because the concept of principle was pragmatically suited to winning the field against the older Tudor-Stuart opportunism in the struggle for men's minds and world markets, though it was necessarily less colorful and heroic in its actions than was the past: "In essentials, the Stuarts' [and Tudors'] cause was picturesque; the Cromwellian [Oliver] cause was a matter of principle. Now a pic-

3. *Ibid.,* p. 284.
4. *Ibid.,* p. 283.

turesque cause may make a very strong and poetic appeal, but it is, after all, a principle that sweeps people away. For poetry is the sublime of common-sense; principle is wrong-headedness wrought up to the sublime pitch. . . ." [5]

It was, concluded Ford, that very vacuity of personality and action in the Puritan dynamic, coupled with its shrewd and pietistic insistence upon principles, that made this new era "the most vital to the evolution of modern England—of the whole modern, Germanized world." [6] In the process it produced those Dutch-Puritan dominant types one sees everywhere in *The "Half-Moon,"* as they roll over more ancient types like Edward Colman who represent the last lingering survivors of the medieval barony. These are the Barons of the Cinque Ports, of whom Colman is the last, most illustrious heir. Unfortunately, like Katherine Howard, he has lived on into an age where he is, by temperament and belief, unable to act effectively. By the end of the novel he dies, having been unable to join forces with the new *Zeitgeist* nor recover the age of aristocracy. With a foot in both camps he suggests that *via media* ever-present in Scott's resolution of historical conflict between past and present. The ameliorations of these contending forces will come in time, but the way is strewn with the inevitable sacrifice of men like Colman—good men and true—which Hegelianism necessarily consigns to the scrap heap. In phrases and sentiments reminiscent of Conrad's own misgivings over historical process, the figure of Hudson in the novel sadly muses on the toll history takes of men like Colman: "I wonder how many good men sleep beneath the waters or little mounds in far countries; or how many true men's bones bleach beneath the suns on sands or grow brittle on frozen ground, leaving widows and the children they have never seen? I trow there are many thousands of them, and thus the world is builded up and spins around." (p. 297)

Ostensibly a tale about Hudson's 1609 voyage to the New World, *The "Half-Moon"* is more concerned with the fate and fortunes of

5. *Ibid.,* p. 285.
6. *Ibid.,* p. 286.

young Edward Colman, a Rye shipbuilder who accompanies Hudson on the voyage. Colman, the last surviving member of the oldest and most illustrious line of the Cinque Ports Barons (Ford stresses their origin in the middle ages), recognizes the declining fortunes and prestige of the ports as "a part of the absolute decay of the Old Faith in England." Impatient with his brother barons who stand ineffectually about recalling their once-privileged position in history, he warns them that theirs is "a newer age," one to which they must adjust or be "lost forever." Before Colman can effectively organize his brother barons, he is forced to flee to Amsterdam as an exile, having been betrayed by a woman jealous of his marriage to a Dutchwoman. Here, hoping for some means of regenerating Ports commerce, he joins Hudson's search for the fabled Northwest Passage. The voyage, plagued by a series of inexplicable misfortunes, comes to nothing as Colman dies in the New World, ostensibly from the arrow of a savage, but in reality from dark and deterministic forces which have pursued him, forces that have their origin in medieval witchcraft and sorcery.

The outlines of Ford's deterministic scheme of history are again recognizable in the telltale faces and figures of his historical characters. Ford apparently conceived of Hudson as an essentially Tudor type of the Holbein paintings, living on into an age where he has become the tool of Dutch-Protestant commercial enterprise, an age of settlement and profit rather than adventure and discovery:

He was a man of great girth, heavy upon his feet, with a square and curly beard of an iron grey and deep-set eyes of a shining black. He had in his air something of the overbearing, something of the masterly, something of the gasconading. . . . He was rather a man of the last age—of Henry's or Elizabeth's day—than of that year of a new century when men were less lusty than he, where men were more prone . . . to form cabals, mutinies and obstinate knots and to question the divine right of pastors and kings. [p. 115]

Facial characteristics in this novel, however, play a less vital part in distinguishing between past and present dominant types than they did in the Tudor trilogy. The reason may simply have been Ford's inability to discover what he regarded as representative portraits for certain periods. Consequently Ford's descriptions of the two sets of conflicting historical personages are done in broader strokes than in the previous historical novels. Opposed to the dark-visaged, jetty-eyed Tudor types are the blond, fair, and blue-eyed Puritan figures. Although James I in his brief appearance displays, as one would expect, the physiognomy of the Tudor heyday with his dark features and "beady bright eyes" (now described as "tired"), the major contrasts in the novel are concentrated in the two women who flank Edward Colman like a pair of Vice and Virtue figures out of medieval drama: Anne Jeal and Magdalena Koop.

Symbolizing respectively the pagan-Catholicism of the remote past and the emergent figure of the fair, blue-eyed Dutch Protestant type, Anne Jeal and Magdalena Koop represent the spirits of English past and English future as they vie for the love of Colman, who represents the uncertain English present. Anne, whose entire orientation is towards a past age, is described as dark and passionate, given to violent rage when her will is thwarted, a woman whose first instinct is to kill the lover who rejects her for the "tall, fair and rosy" Magdalena with her large, blue eyes "apparently passionless and unreflecting," who resembles nothing so much as a Vermeer painting.

Ford's use of dark and light women as temperamental opposites between which the hero must choose recalls Scott's similarly balanced situations in *Ivanhoe* and *The Fortunes of Nigel.* The latter work, set in the same historical period, has for its heroines two women, Margaret and Hermione, one dark and the other light, who represent antithetical temperaments. Scott often had recourse to physiognomy as a method of character delineation—his dark women generally excitable and impatient of social convention, the light-haired inclined to circumspection and prudence. Ordinarily the latter fare better, often marrying the hero, while the dark, more volatile woman usually destroys herself through her violent indifference to social restraint.

With Ford these oppositions are woven into the broader canvas of historical conflict. The dispassionate versus the passionate, fair against dark, Protestant fronting a decadent Catholicism: these are the antitheses of Ford's cultures in conflict, the Time Spirit of one age pitted against that of another. And the prize over which they struggle is England herself, embodied in the figure of Edward Colman. Magdalena's family is the historical representative of the new dominant type, Germanic and dissenting, but recently settled in the old Cinque Ports: merchants dour and silent, but canny and pious. It is Magdalena's father, the Pastor Koop, who saves Edward from falling into the hands of the government bent on striking at the feudal privileges still enjoyed by Colman and his brother Ports barons. With a mind reverent and shrewdly legalistic by turns, Pastor Koop extricates Colman from the warrant-bearing government agents. As the price of his rescue, Colman concedes to the pastor's request that, before fleeing into exile, Colman marry his daughter Magdalena, making over to her all his lands and wealth against the possibility of his death or failure to return. Against this combination of piety and sagacity, Colman concedes to the conditions, though he is already symbolically attracted to the physical and mental type Magdalena represents. The entire scene is Ford's historical cameo of that gradual ascendancy of the Protestant merchant classes of the seventeenth century over the older vested interests already badly crippled by Cromwell's hegemonic policies of the previous century. Even Colman, as we will see, is vaguely aware of the larger historical significance of these events and their portent for the future of England.

Anne Jeal—the dark woman—duped of her lover by the sober craftiness of the Dutch whom she hates, exhibits all the turbulent nature of her medieval heritage, vowing revenge against her hated enemies, with their passive faces and dumb Dutch prayerfulness. Her instruments of revenge—sorcery and necromancy—like her passions and physiognomy, are those of the Dark Ages, described by Ford in *England and the English* as one aspect of "the quasi-Catholic–quasi-Pagan phase of English mediaeval life."[7] Ford makes explicitly clear in the novel his association of Jacobean sorcery with the historical decay of medieval Catholicism, describing Anne Jeal's mumbled incantations as the "backward fragments of Latin prayers of the Old Faith that were all that remained for the most part in England" (pp. 176–77). Anne, both witch and recusant Catholic, calls down "the vengeance of the abolished Saints of Papist days," in shaping a waxen image of her erstwhile lover. Alternately melting her devil's-doll before the fire, whirling peas in a sieve, Anne Jeal, the last representative of a dying order, nonetheless manages to destroy Colman by calling upon the dark crafts of a bygone day.

Flanked by the Vice and Virtue figures of medieval Catholicism and the emerging Protestant dynamic, the protagonist Colman occupies a medial position in the novel. Played upon by the large and deterministic forces of history he reflects that passivity peculiar to so many of Scott's and Ford's heroes. Too far along the evolutionary scale to accept the reactionary doctrines of medieval Catholicism ("Why, as for holy water, I like it not, for I am no papist"), neither can he accept the preachments and melancholy piety of these un-English Dutchmen, who stir his smoldering remembrance of three hundred years of feudal privilege. Cut off equally from past and future Colman is another version of Ford's alien protagonist; born beyond his time and unable to adjust to the new requirements of the age, he is weeded out through the same forces of social and historical selection as Ford's other major protagonists.

That Ford intended his protagonist to be another of those figures caught in the flux of historical change is unmistakable. Temperamentally, his is a house divided against itself, torn by a nostalgia for a lost baronial England with its powers of privilege, yet he is realist enough to recognize the impossibility of his dream, as well as that inevitable modern drift towards efficiency and skepticism:

7. *Ibid.*, p. 289.

And in those days all men, and Edward Colman among them, loved chicanery, sanctuary, and all the differences of life that had come down to them from former days. But . . . that part of him that was modern . . . and sceptical allowed him to see that a foreign Lord Lieutenant, with strong powers behind him, might well disregard the rights of a little and nearly powerless, but very ancient, nest of dwellings. New days had come in . . . with the death of Elizabeth; the newness might well begin to touch Rye town. [pp. 71–72]

Like Norfolk, Gardiner, and the other outmaneuvered reactionaries of the Tudor trilogy, Colman senses the drift of historical change, but is unable or unwilling to accommodate himself to the new spirit —that same sublime wrongheadedness that characterized Katherine Howard before him and Edward Ashburnham after him—and for which we admire all of them the more: that contempt for the merely expedient in the conduct of one's life. Advised that immersion in holy water will break the spell that is draining away his life, he refuses it, savoring as it does of papist superstition. For his refusal to "fight the world with the world's weapons," as Throckmorton once put it to Katherine, he pays with his life.

Against the background of a religious struggle that contains within itself intellectual, psychological, and economic conflict as well, Colman speaks on occasion with the prophetic vision of a *deus ex machina*. The worst breach of objective artistic control comes when Ford permits his protagonist to speak of that far-off day when these contending political forces will settle down into the *via media* of resolved differences of which both Hegel and Scott wrote in their various ways. Ford, writing with the weight of his historical system pressing heavily on his Impressionist's desire for restraint, describes Edward's parting instructions to his aged female servant, herself a fervent Catholic, to whom he has entrusted the safekeeping of his young Dutch-Protestant wife: "She might, he said, if she would, argue with her new mistress upon points of doctrine—Magdalena was no very hot Knipperdolling; but betwixt her pulling one

way and the old woman's pulling the other, Magdalena, or both of
them, might very well come to be of the Church of England, which,
as seemed likely, would remain the Church of that realm for many
years." In its easy and assured prophecy the passage mars the book,
as the reader senses Ford the historical theorist at work, overshadowing Ford the Impressionist artist; and the integrity of action and
character is strained, a fault less observable in the Tudor trilogy.
Because Ford was dealing so nakedly with historical process in *The
"Half-Moon,"* one is struck by a thinness in action and motivation, a
lag between probability and event that shatters the illusion of reality
that was to have been the cornerstone of Impressionist art. Critics
who have traced this weakness to Ford's reliance upon necromancy
and magic as operative forces have ignored the fact that these
elements are but the small and concrete instances of his historical
system at work. It was a recurrent weakness in Ford that even his
most tightly controlled characters must at times step forward and
exhibit a power of analysis for which the reader is in no way
prepared, men who must, as it were, peep out and say to the reader
—no matter how offhandedly—"Oh well, there are large and un-
knowable forces at work here."

In *The "Half-Moon,"* less artfully than in the Tudor novels, Ford
was giving rein to his private, if unoriginal, view of English history.
Contemptuous of a devaluated modernity, the hypocritical and
pious brutality of English imperialism, but with no misoneistic
illusions about the middle ages, Ford was dramatizing in his novels
that growth of the English national spirit, which he had found
described in Green. It was the movement from the warlike temperament of the middle ages, through the moderating but unscrupulous
cunning of the Tudor-Stuart period, to the complacent, moralistic, economically prudent, and wholly unheroic national character
that emerged triumphant with the "Glorious Revolution" and that
formed the basis for the modern spirit. Ford was tracing out in the
world of fiction the cyclical process that inevitably found in the *via
media* the resolution of British social conflict, though the resolution

of those conflicts nearly always requires the sacrifice of noble, generous natures. Out of the struggle between medieval aristocracy, lay and secular, and Tudor absolutism issued the tragedy of Katherine Howard and, a half century later, Edward Colman, the last representative of baronial feudalism and aristocratic power.

Such a conception of English history, with its subsequent indifference to the fate of unusual individuals, understandably shaped Ford's approach to his protagonists in the novels set in the modern scene. To fully appreciate the effectiveness of Ford's historicism as a tool in shaping the alien protagonists of these later novels, one need only glance briefly at *The Benefactor*, published in 1905, before Ford had learned to successfully manipulate his conceptual system in portraying the shift in values between past and present. His first novel after the period of collaboration with Conrad, the book resembles *The Inheritors* in its dramatization of the futility of principled action in twentieth-century society. Foregoing the Wellsian fantasy of *The Inheritors*, the book attempts to deal with the real world on its own terms. Unfortunately these are never clearly delineated through either character or action in any clear or meaningful way. The novel is shrouded in vague ideals, affections, and value assertions, none of which results in any clear commentary on modern values. The objective correlative, simply mischosen in *The Inheritors*, here fails to materialize at all; and the novel must be accounted a failure. If there is any history involved in the novel at all, it is that of the Hueffer family itself. The leading character, George Moffat, open-handed in his imprudent largesse, suggests Ford's own father, who nearly beggared himself with his ill-fated *New Quarterly Review* in attempting to aid promising young artists, a fatal tendency that Ford recognized as well in his maternal grandfather, Madox Brown, and that he himself displayed during his editorship of the *English Review*.

The imprudently generous Moffat, a middle-aged benevolent, has neglected his own small literary gifts and financial well-being in succoring a host of shams, hypocrites, and parasites, whose only return is ingratitude and vilification. A Germanic and late-Victorian gentleman of honor, Moffat exemplifies those characteristics of principle and sentiment carried to the point of self-destruction. Moffat's fatal flaw, though that is too exalted a term, is his tendency to take seriously those Victorian notions to which others simply pay lip-service and really view as exploitable weaknesses. Abandoned by his more prudential wife, mulct of his wealth by his protégées, he befriends a psychotic clergyman named Brede; and while ministering to Brede's paranoia, falls in love with his daughter Clara. When Brede finally subsides into total madness, Moffat, feeling he has earned a measure of repose, determines to go away with the girl. But with the recognition of his own subtle hypocrisy in winning her affections, his marital ties, and their mutually conditioned moral responses of their Victorian fathers, both Moffat and Clara recognize the impossibility of any escape from their heritage. The habit of self-sacrifice is too deeply ingrained in them both, as well as that self-duplicity that is always attendant upon conscious awareness of self-sacrifice. Psychologically crippled by their Victorian heritage, they are incapable of living in the modern world, though there is nothing of the heroic in their failure. They are simply the colorless victims of the shifting *Zeitgeist.*

The novel lacks crisp delineation of that conflict between traditional values and the modern spirit that Ford was to chronicle with increasing sureness, first in his historical novels and gradually those of the modern scene. It lacks as well that driving inevitability of the better works. But the real problem lies with Moffat himself, who fails to generate any interest for the reader. He is, granted, generous and noble, but he lacks the stature—in an Aristotelian sense—of those later protagonists of which he is the pale archetype: the really unusual individual cut off from his proper historical context—the Katherine Howards, Edward Ashburnhams, and Christopher Tietjens, who are always ground down in favor of more normal types. It was only through that conceptual system worked out in his historical fiction that Ford developed a means of commenting on contemporary deterioration in terms of past cultural values. The perfect fusion of historical analyst and social commentator had to await the lessons learned in the writing of the historical novels. *An English Girl* (1907) is Ford's first novel set in the Edwardian era that shows the unmistakable influence of the histories, as it attempts to get at the present national psychology. Unlike *The Benefactor*, it was written after Ford had laid down the basic outline of history in *England and the English*, the Holbein study, and the historical fiction. The *Athenaeum* of March 9, 1907, carried a highly critical review of the Tudor novels, concluding that Ford's talent was unsuited to the historical novel and that he "would probably find a less remote period easier." Six months later a reviewer in the same journal, after reading *An English Girl*, felt compelled to downgrade his colleague's optimism, concluding that Ford had stumbled equally badly with a modern setting and subject, despite an obvious attempt to ape the themes and manner of James. The Jamesian influence on the novel has become a matter of critical consensus and Ford himself readily acknowledged his indebtedness: "The writer [Ford] did attempt two pastiches in the manner of Mr. Henry James, written, one of them, as a variation on a book of essays to give the effect of a tour in the United States—an international affair." [8]

Setting aside the *Athenaeum*'s characteristic antagonism toward all of Ford's work, one must still concede the novel's deficiencies. A prolix attempt to register the moral insouciance of an upper middle-class English family, the novel suffers from thematic irresolution and a dramatic characterization both shifting and tenuous. But as an early attempt at pinpointing the historical cause of increasing cultural torpor, the novel has an intriguingly Hamletesque quality—a surface disorder that nonetheless suggests an underlying design. Its protagonist, Don Kelleg, represents Ford's first full-blown attempt at the alien protagonist in modern dress, a vestigial dominant type

8. Ford Madox Ford, *Joseph Conrad: A Personal Remembrance* (New York, 1965), pp. 186–87.

from an earlier historical epoch. In his moral and ethical estrangement amidst a post–Boer War society he flounders helplessly in the self-same historical predicament as Katherine Howard and Edward Colman earlier; only the historical setting has changed. Like them his inevitable failure becomes an oblique commentary on the society that destroys him. The difficulty is that this increasingly stock figure in Ford's fiction is almost unrecognizable in the context of the novel's Jamesian veneer of an international affair.

The plot centers about a young American expatriate during the first decade of the twentieth century. Idealistic and artistic by temperament, he has purposely estranged himself from his family's commercial empire and his father, who presides over it. In reaction he has become a quasi-successful illustrator for some of the better English magazines and engaged to an English girl, Eleanor Greville, whom he has met while studying in Paris and to whom he attributes his own awakening sensibility. His sole concern, as the novel opens, is to submerge himself in her individual values and those of her class and family, divorcing himself even more completely from his American heritage. His resolution quickly fades upon learning he has become the heir to his father's commercial empire in America. The thin veneer of his self-imposed Hellenism peels away to reveal a stout layer of Hebraism underneath, James's "New England Conscience." Ford actually uses the term at one point in the novel, while speaking in his narrative voice of his protagonist's nature.

The upshot of Don's newly discovered social conscience is his compulsive pilgrimage to America, where he attempts to rectify the social abuses of his father's commercial freebootery. In a series of slow-moving, talky scenes (with divisions much like those of James), Kelleg discovers progressively that he is not the person he took himself for and that the problem of economic restitution for his father's social misdeeds is inordinately more complex than he had supposed. Depressed by his inability to dissolve his father's commercial empire and sickened by the unaesthetic sledgehammers of Fifth Avenue, Don retreats to England, intending once again to submerge himself in the values of Eleanor and of the class she represents. Blood tells, however, and his social conscience drives him back to America as the novel closes.

Kelleg, Ford seems to be saying, has sought to embrace a way of life for which he is temperamentally unsuited, for he is not of this class, nor even of these times—as Eleanor's father is forever pointing out to anyone who will listen. The novel chronicles one of Ford's usual struggles for self-knowledge by a protagonist placed in an alien culture where he is temperamentally unable to function or even able to make himself understood. And in this sense Don Kelleg represents another of Ford's deracinated young heroes out of touch with the spirit of his age. At the same time, his role as cultural outsider provided Ford with an alien persona from which to view the modern scene.

Kelleg's similarity to earlier types in Ford's fiction has been noted by a number of critics, among them Richard Cassell, who early argued that "Don Kelleg, though thoroughly American in his confidence in the future, and in his energetic quest for new idealistic worlds, is an extension of the earlier protagonists into a savior of mankind." [9] Now Kelleg, whose failure is as complete as can be imagined, hardly qualifies as a "savior" in much other than desire; and if he is an extension of anything, it is of Ford's dominant historical type which had come on the world's stage at the time of the Puritan, but is ill at ease in the twentieth century, like that late protagonist of Ford, Henry Martin of *The Rash Act*, who attributes his failure to the fact that though he was born in the nineteenth century, he has lived most of his life in the twentieth. Kelleg is much more specifically linked to the sentimental and moralistic values of the Puritan dominant type, though familiarity with Victorian affluence has dissolved the acquisitiveness of his Puritan heritage. Even his name suggests his national origins and ethnic background.

9. Richard A. Cassell, *Ford Madox Ford: A Study of His Novels* (Baltimore, 1961), p. 119.

The novel suffers in being overfreighted with a concern for social values—values whose source is never made clear and which blur confusingly into one another. The primary cause is the inordinate difficulty of picking one's way through the welter of conflicting and blurring social values dramatized or expressed through various characters. Some cancel each other out; others contradict one another; and still others seem to come to nothing by the novel's end, including the moralistic and reforming zeal of the protagonist himself.

These weaknesses are inevitably reflected in the paucity of dramatic conflict. Where the conflicts of the Tudor novels were realized in a straightforward struggle between opposed dominant types, Katherine and Cromwell, there is no clear-cut opposition in the issues raised in the action of *An English Girl*. One senses the disparity of temperament between Kelleg and his fiancée and father-in-law, but there is not that sense of malignant resistance between ages in conflict one finds in the Tudor trilogy, nor even that opposition of cultures exemplified in Newman's encounter with the Bellegarde family, James's early use of the international theme Ford was trying to combine with his own myth of successive historical types. As a matter of fact, all of the characters in *An English Girl* are on the side of the protagonist, even those whose cultural values, like Grenville and Canzano, are most antithetical to his own. Consequently where a Katherine Howard struggled against real adversaries in a highly dramatic context, Don Kelleg struggles against nothing more tangible than his own inanition and confusion. Nor is there any breakthrough towards the self-understanding earlier protagonists won for themselves. But the little Don does gain of self-understanding comes not at all to his fiancée, Eleanor Greville; and the novel is a severe indictment of her particular English class, which had been the fairest game for the social criticism of Carlyle and Arnold in the preceding generation, and which both Ford and Forster were still pursuing on Edwardian ground.

Though Kelleg once refers to the "sort of semi-socialist ideals" in which he, like Ford, had been brought up, the gospel he preaches is that of Arnold and Carlyle, which James had rarified into his own international theme, partly as a result of Arnold's having exaggerated the importance of Puritan stock in America, fixing upon New Englanders especially the reputation of a scrupulously Hebraic mentality. Ford, accepting this popular fallacy, made it a part of his own outline of history, maintaining that America had preserved the old Protestant dynamic, that moral vigor that was the supposed legacy of Puritanism, but refined down to the emphasis upon "Principle" after the glorious revolution and the installation of the archetype of the Dutch-Protestant spirit, William III.[10] Edward Colman in *The "Half-Moon,"* Ford's historical prophet, had predicted this spirit would pass to the New World leaving England to suffer from the hypocrisy of principles divorced from life, which to Ford had been the stock and legacy of the Victorian national temper.

Kelleg, like Colman, represents a partial reconciliation of opposed forces, here those of Hebraist and Hellenist. And he has the suitably symbolic parentage—an English mother and an American father. Having inherited characteristics of both cultures, he discovers quickly enough he fits into neither. He does possess that same "remarkably developed moral sense" Ford thought characteristic of the seventeenth-century Dutch-Protestant dynamic, hence his symbolic name. To the modern Englishman like Greville, who suffers from the national declension of the spirit, Don seems, as Greville says, "unreasonably kind," lacking in "any kind of system in his morality." The implication is that "system" is all the modern-day Englishman has left to him, the heart of a once strong ethical and religious conviction having passed over to the New World as Colman had prophesied it would, and as Kelleg—hawking Ford's historical evolutionism—also prophesies. Attacking his father's roughshod business tactics as retrograde and noting Europe's loss of vital energy, Kelleg preaches Ford's favorite theory of the progressive "Time Spirit": "It [his father's unprincipled actions] is not in the

10. *England and the English*, p. 290.

irit of the time. It's a survival. It is not—it is not. What America's
?re for is to carry the thing one step further: to do what Europe is
? tired to do. . . . It is not in the spirit of their times: it is not in
spirit of yours. He's an accident—a phenomenon such as my
1er and his fellows." (p. 15) In Ford's sweeping view of history it
is America that has maintained the old Protestant dynamic with its
concern for principled action, while the impulse had largely died
out in the enervated middle classes of England, whose major representative (Don's father-in-law) yawns, "It's not much good trying
to redress the burdens of our ancestry" (p. 13). But he labors under
that overwhelming Judaic conscience that refuses to let him sit idle
and affluent.

With a bare touch of artistic talent Kelleg has the requisite
aesthetic appreciation of the fine and the good, exemplified in the
easy, cultured life of the Grevilles; on the other hand, he is imbued
with the moral activist's impulse to strike a blow at the social
inequities created by his father's commercial empire, his American
Hebraistic legacy. "Heaven knows," he says, "it's not power that's
given me. It's a burden; it's a duty." (p. 13) The enervated Grevilles
treat his fervor as interesting and harmless quixotism. Though he
embodies the desired norm of Hebraism and Hellenism, neither
England nor American has any real place for him; and it is here that
Ford superimposes his own concept of alien protagonist and cultural
outsider upon James's international theme: a Newman or Isabel
Archer at least fits someplace. But the protagonist of *An English
Girl* is himself finally driven to realize that in this world he has no
place, that he hangs, as he says, "suspended between heaven and
earth, like Mahomet's coffin."

With its heavy surcharge of Arnoldian social criticism, *An English Girl* challenges the same weaknesses of Edwardian society that
Forster attacks in *Howards End,* published three years later in 1910.
Both novels explore the relationship between the life of cultured
leisure and the commercial energy that makes that life possible. Both
aim towards the *via media* as a resolution of these antithetical forces

in society, Forster in the figure of the child born to Leonard and Helen, Ford in the fused values of his disjunctive hero.

Though Kelleg, as the novel opens, has tried to submerge himself in a cultural setting for which he is but partially suited, he experiences the same conflict that put Katherine Howard so at odds with her society. And like her he suffers from a lack of self-understanding, an endemic weakness among Ford's heroes. Still, Kelleg resembles the heroine of the earlier novels less closely than he does Robert Grimshaw of *A Call*, a later figure he in many ways anticipates, even as he does Edward Ashburnham of *The Good Soldier*. The conception of all three owes a good deal more than has been recognized to Ford's concept of historical evolution. Each of these figures, because he initially misreads his own nature, brings, at best, sorrow and anguish, at worst, tragedy to himself and those about him through his idealistic and ingenuous bumbling.

Greville, Ford's on-the-scene analyst, recognizes and warns of this tendency in the protagonist's character: "If a man is determined to inflict himself on his times it is his duty first to consider what *he* is! For what is criminal is to wobble once you have begun. A man has to define what his ideal is and then to make for it. . . . You'll do less harm if you let things alone. But you'll do infinitely more if, once you've begun to meddle, you change your mind." (p. 127) But because he belongs to the dominant psychological type that came into being with the seventeenth century, the "tall, fair-haired" Dutch Protestant strain with its "ingenuous" and "sentimental" attitude toward a life based on principle, Kelleg cannot desist. Representative of that last dwindling strain of nineteenth-century altruism, he insists on trying to impose his prescriptive values on a world and time he barely understands. Again, it is Greville, Ford's peripatetic *deus ex machina*, who explains Don's puzzling incapacity to function in the present:

The place of such men was gone from the world. What decent men there were in public life today did more harm than good, and they soiled themselves by mixing in pettiness.

"And," he added, "that's what will be the trouble with Don. He's too decent—in an idealist, impractical way—to handle the problems here. He won't even begin to understand them." And Mr. Greville said that, for the convenience of speaking, he'd say that Don was a nineteenth-century altruist. . . . [p. 237]

Scattered throughout Ford's novels are these strange and peculiar little judgments upon the fitness or unfitness of a man's personality for the times he finds himself in. Spoken by commentators who stand outside the main action of the novel, they give repeated testimony to Ford's historical assumption "that in the history of the world as among man there have always been psychological ages." [11]

For the remainder of the novel, as Kelleg fumbles progressively on the modern scene, Ford, through his analyst-commentator Greville, simply reiterates that Don is "hopelessly out of date with his time" (p. 267). Early critics saw in this particular modern protagonist simply one more of Ford's vaguely medieval gentlemen, a modern man who "obviously wished for an ideal code like feudalism . . . ," [12] or who was said to be "a believer in a rural, pseudo-medieval, aristocratic world. . . ." [13] A bare glance at Ford's outline of psychological evolution, as he explains it in *England and the English*, will serve to prove how little Ford conceived of Don Kelleg as a medieval type. Such criticism suffers by working backward from the character of Ashburnham in *The Good Soldier*, a figure who undoubtedly has strongly marked medieval traits. But Kelleg has none of them—in temper, physique, or facial characteristics; he belongs to a later age.

But the precise origins of Ford's intruder from the past are of less moment than the critical use he is intended to serve, a satiric counter against which may be measured the collapsing values of Edwardian society. A product of that evolving national Time Spirit that turns

11. *Ibid.*, p. 278.
12. Elliott B. Gose, "The Strange Irregular Rhythm: An Analysis of *The Good Soldier*," *PMLA*, LXXII (June, 1957), 509.
13. R. W. Lid, "Tietjens in Disguise," *The Kenyon Review*, XXII (Spring, 1960), 268.

up its occasional tragic anomolies, Kelleg exhibits all the values and convictions of the previous age, virtues to which the Edwardian age has gone dead. Though his failure is inevitable, it is also a reminder to the reader (whom Ford wishes to show where he stands) of what has been lost to the world in its secular hurrying through space. But the technique was still imperfect; this dilemma of the principled man in an unprincipled society was inadequately geared to Ford's social diagnostics.

If the resolution of *An English Girl* seems muddy, as indeed it does, the reason lies in the fact that Ford's particular type of protagonist fits poorly within the context of the Jamesian international theme, based as the latter is on those arbitrary categories introduced by Carlyle and sophisticated by Arnold. In Ford's novel class characteristics, individual psychology, cultural diversity, and social evolution have all sifted down to one rather muddy residuum. *An English Girl* can only be accounted an ambitious failure in Ford's earliest attempt at depicting the post-Victorian breakup in terms of his alien protagonist, though it represents an undeniable advance over *The Benefactor*. Don Kelleg, Ford's first quasi-successful modern protagonist, achieves a stature greater than George Moffat of *The Benefactor*, who fails in the face of indifference and ingratitude. Kelleg, with his activist spirit, flings himself, however ineffectually, against the tenor of the times; but he falls between the two stools of the Anglo-American world. He is that extension of Ford's earlier historical misfit, the protagonist poised between two worlds, unable to come to ground in either. He represents an improvement over the figure of Moffat, being far more effective as a satiric contrast to present values—and he is a recognizable anticipation of Colman in *The "Half-Moon,"* another man caught between two worlds.

Between the appearance of *The Benefactor* in 1905 and *The "Half-Moon"* in 1909 came the Tudor trilogy and two other novels with a contemporary setting, *An English Girl* (1907) and *Mr. Apollo* (1908). *Mr. Apollo*, another attempt at suggesting a viable alternative to Edwardian opulence and material glut, marks a temporary reversion to Wellsian fantasy. The novel contains a brief suggestion of the cyclic evolution lying in the background of the histories and *An English Girl*. The Greek god Apollo, having returned to the present, describes from his timeless perspective the rise and fall of Western generations. As in *The Inheritors*, Ford has turned a Wellsian occurrence to the purposes of social satire. But the attempt to give the Edwardian reader a perspective from which to view contemporary secular complacency fails—for much the same reason it failed in *The Inheritors*. The central device of the novel, Apollo's supernatural disquisitions on the proper nature of man, neutralizes the tone of social realism and moral concern. Apollo is literally the *deus ex machina*, with all the traditional weaknesses inherent in the device; and his other-worldly presence destroys his technical function in the novel—that of a realistic counter against which Edwardian social shortcomings might be measured. The cultural alternatives are prosily clear, but there is not that sense of values in conflict better dramatized in the historical contestants of the Tudor novels.

Suggestions of Ford's cyclicalism are in evidence, but Ford never weaves them into the warp and woof of human events; they are simply superimposed by the oracular commentary of Apollo, who warns of history's lesson, the same lesson voiced by Ford in *England and the English* as well as in *The Inheritors*, and later echoed in Yeats's vision: that the world can reel backwards into barbarism under the corrosive influence of materialistic imperialism. In a central statement of theme it is Apollo who recalls to his Edwardian listeners the cyclical theories of Egathistotheopompus, that ancient philosopher and prophet of Rome's decline and fall: "He it was who especially had promulgated the theory that mankind was not perfectible, but moved in cycles, that there had been a Golden Day in Egypt that declined, till in Athens the wheel of humanity was again exalted, and so in Rome, and so doubtless onwards into the unknown future and back into the unchronicled past." [14] Ford hoped, though with decreasing confidence, that the spectacle of what he called "ferocity" discernible in the English national temper during the Boer war was but a short-lived phenomenon. But the novel is less concerned with this possibility than with the very evident moral erosion of the old German-Protestant spirit born in the seventeenth century but dying at the close of the nineteenth.

The one character who stands out as the antithesis of the ethical humanism preached by the Mediterranean god is Mr. Todd, the final and degenerate strain of the Protestant spirit, of which Ford wrote in *England and the English:* "Philosophically . . . it began that divorce of principle from life which, carried as far as it has been carried in England, has earned for the English the title of a nation of hypocrites." [15] And so it is that Apollo, in justifiable and godly rancor, turns this last representative of debased Puritanism into a bay tree, in Ford's mind a suitably ironic fate for the great enemy of all that is good in art and life. But as Ford amused himself taking revenge on the tribe of Gosson, his art suffered accordingly. There can be no sense of sympathy or human dignity, no matter how correct his values, for an alien protagonist who turns adversaries into bay trees at will or who, unlike Katherine Howard or Edward Ashburnham, need not pay with his life for his unfashionable principles. Thus comes that pronounced failure in the satiric tone of the novel, a failure not unlike that of *Ladies Whose Bright Eyes.* Nor can this failure be excused by the extended range of Ford's social criticism, which breaks beyond the narrow circle of *The Benefactor* and *An English Girl* and anticipates that greater breadth of focus in *Mr. Fleight.* There Ford exposes the universal folly of all levels of Edwardian society and the novel structure is correspondingly better framed to enclose the satiric panorama. And the panorama itself is seen through the temperamental lens of a more believable alien

14. Ford Madox Ford, *Mr. Apollo: A Just Possible Story* (London, 1908), p. 48.
15. *England and the English*, p. 290.

persona—the monied Jew of Edwardian society. Ford, in *Mr. Apollo*, was moving toward a set of cultural values located outside the Anglo-American scene of *An English Girl* and away from the medieval world view of the early historical novels. Although *A Call* lies in this line of development, *Mr. Apollo* shows Ford first turning his attention to the cultural and temperamental disparity between northern and southern Europe, that Nordic-Latinate dichotomy that by the end of his life was codified into the geo-cultural myths of *Provence* and *Great Trade Route*. Apollo, as a representative of the southern, rather than northern panoply of gods, stands for the cultural and communal values traditionally associated with the Mediterranean world. The ethical values preached by Apollo in the novel are those Ford offers as an alternative to the secular materialism of the north European, the final residue of the northern Protestant dynamic. Despite the rigorous austerity of its birth in Calvin and Knox there soon came that early confusion of ethical conduct and material success that typifies the Dutch-Protestant community of *The "Half-Moon."* In his search for a synthesis of the Nordic and Latinate mentalities in *A Call*, Ford again turned to the protagonist poised between the cultural systems of two unlike worlds, separated not by time—as in the Tudor histories and *The "Half-Moon"*—but by geography, somewhat after the manner of Don Kelleg in *An English Girl*.

# 5. Variations on a Theme

What finally distinguishes Ford from other Edwardian novelists—Conrad, James, Forster, Galsworthy—are those protean turns and twists of experimentiveness, that zigzag pattern of theme, setting, and technique that characterizes his work up until 1915. By comparison there is a predictable sameness in the early work of his contemporaries, particularly Forster, and even Conrad until he turned inward from the sea. Ford's willingness to experiment, seeking always that popular audience that seemed to elude both him and James, is nowhere better illustrated than in the variant clothes in which he draped his alien protagonist. Although the suits and trappings of this figure borrow heavily from James and Forster, for example, the underlying pattern of conflict remained uniquely Ford's own—born of that persistent, in some ways adolescent, yearning for the lost ideals, personal and public, of that mythic Golden Age to which his protagonist always harks back.

His attempted modulation of the Jamesian international theme shortly gave way to a Forster-like exploration of the ideals of the Mediterranean cultures as a possible corrective to the decadent culture of northern Europe. Anything in these years seemed grist for his mill, which ground too fast perhaps to produce any really lasting work. Sometime in the early spring of 1909, Ford struck out after that bright new phoenix of Edwardian fiction, the psychological novel. Critics have unanimously and rightly acclaimed *A Call*, published in 1910, as Ford's first really subtle psychological examination of the breakdown of England's old ruling class under the corrosive influence of idleness, nerves, and affluence. All the major characters suffer quietly the conflict between personal passion and restrictive social conventions, but none more acutely than the protagonist Robert Grimshaw. Although his relationship to his social milieu is as uneasy as Katherine Howard's or Don Kelleg's, Grimshaw is Ford's first experiment with those interracial figures who represent an alternative cultural tradition lying outside the Anglo-Saxon world, though still in the present age.

Robert Grimshaw, an Anglo-Greek living comfortably on the upper fringes of London society, is another of Ford's typically alienated central characters. Ostensibly a member of the traditionally governing class, he has withdrawn from active engagement in politics, content to sit in the shadows and direct the lives and careers of younger men. His hand-picked disciple, Dudley Leicester, is wealthy, otiose, and hypochondriacal, the last sad spasm of England's ruling strain. Under Grimshaw's tutelage he is transformed into a quasi-competent landlord and potential member of Parliament, a political leader whose role—as Grimshaw conceives it—will be to shore up the collapsing beams of their class structure. To assist in his project of reclamation, Grimshaw marries his pupil to an impeccable, and supposedly superficial, young woman drawn from their own class. She is Pauline Lucas, a woman of unexpected spunk, intelligence, and resiliency, whom Grimshaw secretly loves and is loved by in return. Perpetuation of their class, reasons Grimshaw, comes first, and with proper British reserve he coldly hands her over to Leicester. Unfortunately Grimshaw's long-repressed Latinate temperament, the genetic inheritance of his Greek ancestry, revolts at such emotional self-mutilation, further darkening an ego already clouded by self-delusion and unnatural restraint.

Grimshaw's deterioration, hastened by repressed sexual jealousy, drives him into an unconscious and paranoic hatred of his young friend, who he wrongly imagines is having a clandestine affair. With unconscious fury Grimshaw subtly torments his former protégé, playing on an already exhausted nervous system, finally driving Leicester into a state of catatonic shock. As the portrait of a class with nerves strained to the breaking point, the novel obviously anticipates those "screaming hysterics" of which Dowell sadly speaks in the opening pages of *The Good Soldier*. The last chapters of *A Call* trace Grimshaw's growing self-knowledge and subsequent sense of guilt. As Leicester's condition worsens, the protagonist realizes too late that through having repressed his own Latinate emotionalism he has condemned to mental purgatory his wholly innocent friend whose only crime was to lend himself to Grimshaw's misguided and messianic impulse to perpetuate a governing tradition already a matter of history. To accomplish his ends, Grimshaw, who in his own personality suggests the causes of the cultural dissolution, had sought to embrace the English aristocrat's codes and conventions, ones for which he is temperamentally unsuited.

Although Grimshaw represents a variation of that remote persona from behind which Ford sought to underscore the altering complexion of the English national temperament, the conception of his dilemma is a natural development of Ford's earlier technique, now influenced by those rediscovered theories of racial psychology that had appeared in Victorian literature as early as *Daniel Deronda* but were still as current as Forster and Edwardian racial theory. It was upon these theories that Ford was to rely increasingly heavily in novels like *A Call* and *Mr. Fleight* and that formed the central assumptions of that late impressionistic travelogue *Great Trade Route*, his final cultural analysis of the West, published two years before his death. Leisurely, philosophical, and intensely prophetic, *Great Trade Route* was the parable Ford spun out at the end of his days, a summing up as deeply somber in theme and intent as Wells's *Mind at the End of Its Tether*.

Where the Tudor novels had depended exclusively upon Ford's historical theories as a *sub rosa* explanation of their human conflicts, *Great Trade Route* relied upon ethnic and nationalistic determinism as an explanation of temperamental oppositions among men. *Great Trade Route* constitutes Ford's final statement of his cultural and racial theories. In the book Ford argues an unending temperamental opposition between conflicting Nordic and Latinate personality "types." De-emphasizing his old conceptual system built on successive historical cycles, Ford imagines a latitudinal boundary circumscribing the world along which exists a continuing warfare between the land to the north and that to the south, worlds that have evolved differently: agrarianism as opposed to industrialism, small producerism versus technocracy, communalism versus militarism. In each instance it is the former Ford values and sees preserved only in the cultures of the Mediterranean area. Equally obvious is the resemblance of this southern culture to the values Ford had originally associated with the medieval world, with the exception of those pacifistic tendencies he attributes to nations south of the fortieth parallel. The final tableau is a highly imaginative, deeply personal *Weltanschauung*, by which Ford sought once again to schematize the bewildering flux of the modern world—as that world appeared to Ford in 1937, on the eve of the war whose military alignments were to shatter his myth.

Ford did not discard the ideals of his beloved medievalism; instead he imagined he saw them still operative in the Mediterranean world of the twentieth century, an area of the Western world that had retained intact most of the ideals and traditions of aristocratic leadership lost to the north of Europe, a loss to which Grimshaw repeatedly alludes in the novel: "They [the English] can work; they can fight; they can do things; but it is for themselves alone. They're individualists. But there is a class that's got the sense of duty to the whole. They've got a rudimentary sense of it—a tradition, at least, if not a sense. But the tradition's dying out."[1] Grimshaw realizes that this sort of Nordic laissez-faire individualism, superficially sanctioned by social Darwinism—and dramatized by Forster as the Wilcox mentality—is inimical to a responsible and interdependent society, the sort of thing one finds in the south of Europe with its continuing feudal traditions. Acknowledging his biracial heritage and subsequent alien temperament, Grimshaw notes his unlikeness to his half-brother Englishmen: " 'I suppose,' Robert Grimshaw said speculatively, 'it's because I'm really Greek. My name's English, and my training's been English, and I look it, and smell it, and talk it, and dress the part; but underneath I should think I'm really a Dago. You see, I'm much more my mother's child than my father's. She was a Lascarides, and that's a clan name. Belonging to a clan makes you have what no Englishman being Nordic has—a sense of responsibility.' " (pp. 163–64) Being half-Greek Grimshaw does have this active sense, the southern and Catholic concept of individual and cultural totality; but he has another side as well: the Nordic, dissident, and individualistic sense, born of Puritanism and Germanic technocracy, which to Ford was the most ominous social phenomenon of the twentieth century.

As a phenotype of the Mediterranean-Latinate-feudal civilization, but raised and educated in England, Grimshaw functions in the novel much as does Edward Colman in *The "Half-Moon"* and Don Kelleg in *An English Girl* or even Katherine Howard in the Tudor novels, all somehow misplaced in their milieu. Whereas Katherine is a medieval type unable to function in a later period of English history, Grimshaw is at odds with his society because, as a representative of the Mediterranean culture—where feudal-like values persist —he is equally out of touch with the modern world of northern Europe. Like Ford's earlier protagonists, Grimshaw stands poised between divided and distinguished worlds. Although Kelleg it is

1. Ford Madox Ford, *A Call: The Tale of Two Passions* (London, 1910), p. 178. (All subsequent references will be to this edition.)

true is characterized as a nineteenth-century altruist unable to perform satisfactorily in present-day America, he, like Grimshaw, has violated one half of his hereditary temperament. The development in Ford's mental picture of the "mundane cosmogony" seems fairly clear, though it is unlikely that it had been carefully thought out. One suspects that, like Topsy, it "just growed," the unphilosophic artist's response to the problem of explaining society to itself in terms it finds most meaningful at the moment. And in the late Edwardian period this meant ethnology and psychology rather than history.

Whereas the early alien protagonists are manufactured from Ford's historical system, and though it never really disappears from his assumptions, the emphasis in *An English Girl* begins to shift towards an ethnological explanation of the protagonist's alienation. The process continues into *A Call*, where the same type of cultural dichotomy is expressed in terms of Freudian dualism, Grimshaw's opposed conscious and subconscious concerns; and so it has been called a psychological novel; but it was really a case of new wine in an old bottle—the old myth of successive psychological ages through history. Only the case now was that occasionally an age might survive reasonably intact, as with the Mediterranean-feudal world order. Sometime between the Tudor novels and *An English Girl* Ford had become disenchanted with the "New England conscience" as a desirable corrective for that greater evil, the English *malaise*. And by the end of his life he had decided that "the New England conscience or states . . . at present seem to me to be the most detestable things in the world and the source of all our present evils." [2] And the undertones in *An English Girl* had pointed to Ford's growing association of medieval values with contemporary Mediterranean civilization. The Italian Count Canzano, a secondary character who occupies an ambiguous position in the novel, seems

2. Ford Madox Ford, *Great Trade Route* (New York and Toronto, 1937), p. 194.

vaguely intended as a foil to the protagonist's anguished soul-searching in a world of chimeric values. In him, as Paul Wiley early recognized, "lie vestiges of an older Catholic tradition of positive right and wrong which give poise to his gaiety and enable him to maintain his own form of balance in the conflicts of contemporary existence."[3] Still the values represented by Canzano provide no corrective for the protagonist's temperamental conflict with the age. And despite that awkward postscript at the end of *A Call*, the novel offers no tangible reconciliation between the Nordic and Latinate world views, the sort of *via media* hinted at in the earlier historical novels.

In the next-to-last novel he wrote, *Henry for Hugh* (1934), is Ford's last fictional dramatization of his Nordic-Latinate myth. Henry Smith, ostensibly a Nordic but with Latinate yearnings and tastes, is elated to discover at the end of the novel that he really has "no Anglo-Saxon blood." In essence the novel stresses the idea of the Mediterranean race's sense of joy and pleasure in the world, as opposed to the austere and efficiency-minded north Europeans; and in one rather talky scene a character lectures the protagonist on the essential differences between the two types. In the course of the explanation she refers symbolically to the "bridge" that one day may unite the two types, but such a possibility is left in the remote future. Ford, like Forster, after posing the problem of communication between unlike minds often skirts the problem of resolution. And in *A Call* no sort of workable reconciliation is suggested, primarily because Ford was presenting the problem of diverse cultural temperaments in terms of individual psychology based on racial characteristics and Freudian repression. Grimshaw suffers mental conflict as a result of his biracial ancestry, and in his ambivalence mirrors Ford's larger theme of racial antithesis.

Ford's own approach to race and culture was that of the imagina-

3. Paul Wiley, *Novelist of Three Worlds: Ford Madox Ford* (Syracuse, N.Y., 1962), p. 150.

tive amateur. Lacking either tools or inclination for cranial measurement—then in vogue among Edwardian ethnologists—Ford chose to consider race simply as a matter of geographic locale and of national spirit. In seeking to define the Anglo-Saxon attitude Ford once wrote, "It is not . . . a matter of race but one, quite simply, of place —of place and of spirit, the spirit being born of the environment." [4] Even during his years of semi-isolation at Pent Cottage, Ford was always sensitive to currents and modes in the English novel, leading him to overfreight his plots, as he does with both *An English Girl* and *A Call*. With *A Call* he sought to tap that popular audience made psychology-conscious through the work of William and Henry James, as well as the writings and public lectures of Freud and Morton Prince. Ford welded James's delicate exfoliations of guilt and repression together with his own personal myth of racial and temperamental conflict.

The course of Grimshaw's psychological deterioration derives directly from his biracial ancestry. Half-English, half-Greek, he has driven underground his passionate southern nature—the part that loved Pauline Lucas; and he retains only the Latinate sense of communal responsibility he seeks to instill into Dudley Leicester. Having by now mastered the use of the *progression d'effet*, Ford strews a broadening path of hints—image, analogy, allusion—to suggest some concealed self-contradiction behind Grimshaw's surface attitudes. Facial characteristics, as in the historical novels, again play an important part in signaling the temperamental nature of the characters. Grimshaw resembles "a Levantine pirate," a south European of an earlier, more heroic age. And his cousin Ellida, said to resemble him, is described as that "slim, dark and passionate girl with . . . the dark eyes," a girl of whom it was said "there was no knowing what religion might not have done for this Southern nature . . ." (p. 23). What really gives Grimshaw away are those unex-

4. Ford Madox Ford, *England and the English: An Interpretation* (New York, 1907), p. 263.

pected emotional outbursts at moments of shock and stress when the superimposed veneer of his public-school training peels back, revealing the Greek underside of his personality. During a scene of deep emotional restraint as Grimshaw goes to the railway station to see off on her honeymoon the woman he secretly loves, Pauline Lucas hurls to the platform a bouquet of violets he hands her. After a moment's shocked silence, he crushes them violently beneath his heel; then as the train departs, he gathers them up, muttering over them a spell taught him by his old Greek nurse as a child, a spell intended to bind another's love to himself. Horrified, his cousin reproaches him for lapsing back into the old ways of their people. Momentarily overcome by his long repressed Latin passions, he resorts to pagan superstition and ritual to undo the work of his English alter ego—that of coolly handing over the woman he desires to another man. Grimshaw betrays his kinship with those tempestuous medieval characters who appear in Ford's early historical fiction. He has the passions, countenance, and occult disposition of Anne Jeal, that earlier throwback to the deep past. The best example of Ford's association of necromancy with the middle ages, perhaps the combined influence of Green and his own brother's researches, comes through most strongly in his novel *The Young Lovell* (1913).

A surrealistic tale set in the middle ages, *The Young Lovell* moves across a landscape mingling fays and spirits amidst the graphic realism of Pre-Raphaelite detail, leading critics to dismiss it as juvenile fiction. To say that this is a mistake is not to argue that it is a good novel; it is not. But its importance for this study lies in the fact that it is Ford's first fictional statement of his belief in the kindred nature of the medieval and Hellenic spirit. At the close of the novel the young knight Lovell undergoes one of those characteristic splinterings of personality so frequent in Ford—even in those late novels like *When the Wicked Man, The Rash Act, Vive Le Roy,* and *Henry for Hugh.* Lovell, after the successful siege in which he recaptures his ancestral castle, mysteriously disappears from the scene. His physical self retires to a hermit's cave for the remainder of his life, while his "spirit," for lack of a better word, is wafted to a mountainous isle in the Mediterranean, vaguely recognizable as Olympus. Here, under the admiring eyes of "the fairy lady"—actually Venus—who had pursued him across a medieval English landscape, he wiles away eternity jousting with Mars, the god of war. Here, in these Mediterranean climes, at any rate, all that was best in the age of chivalry will endure. A strange novel, it seems almost a fictional dream of wish fulfillment.

Grimshaw's Mediterranean heritage and pagan spirit are but a pale reminder of the color and turbulence with which Ford invested the medieval scene, but by now time had rolled its hump some five hundred years onward. And Grimshaw, in a rare philosophical moment, recognizes the waning spirit of his race, that their blood had run progressively thinner since his ancestors simply seized and held that which they desired—whether land or woman. Confessing his polygamous instincts—sadly at variance with his public-school education—he says to his cousin: " 'I suppose what I really want is both Katya and Pauline. That sort of thing is probably in our blood —yours and mine—and no doubt in the great days of our race I should have had both of them, but I've got to sacrifice physical possession of one of them to the amenities of civilization . . . that's taken thousands of years to bring together. We're the children of that age.' " (p. 34)

This truism of man's animal instincts hemmed in by social restraint was an increasingly popular theme with Edwardian novelists, a situation as old and older than Chaucer but given new immediacy by Buckle's essays on the taming of the human spirit and Freud's description of the "primal horde." If one is to judge on the basis of his novels and what goes on in them, Ford unquestionably saw contemporary social convention as a less powerful impulse behind human action than those ethnic characteristics over which man can exert but minimal control. The psychological conflict within Grimshaw—worked out in Ford's private Nordic-Mediterranean myth— was simply one more novelist's explanation of the subrational in human nature erupting in an age and society that both incites one to revolt and punishes one for it. That new Edwardian emphasis upon irrational motivation is what ultimately lies behind the network of farce and tragedy in Conrad's *The Secret Agent,* for which Ford apparently supplied the central circumstances; and there are those continual whispers of it in Galsworthy—that "primeval impulse," the brute welling up, in Soames Forsyte that continually urges him against social restraint. And even before Freud and Prince, Edwardians and late Victorians had been alerted to the frightening possibility of subterranean forces within the mind itself through Constance Garnett's translations of Dostoevsky.

But with Ford the new vogue for psychological and irrational motivation was interwoven with his increasing reliance upon popular ideas of ethnology, which, like psychology itself, was simply one more version of the late-Victorian notion of "process." Consequently *A Call* must be read at both the allegorical and the individual level, in much the same manner as *Parade's End.* Both chronicle, and it is not too strong a verb, the inadequacy and subsequent collapse of traditional values in the modern world; both underscore the part played by a political paralysis literally based on madness, a governing class inbred to the point of extermination, the secularization of religious impulse, and—that surest index of Edwardian concern—the fragmented personality.

Grimshaw, despite the mental wars within him, is concerned to perpetuate those values so meaningful to Christopher Tietjens and, in his less self-conscious way, Edward Ashburnham: a feudal world of ordered and hierarchic interdependence, given form and sanction by a solid community of religious belief. It was the elusive, often destructive, grail they all pursued, and a sad reminder in Ford of those repinings Richard Aldington once noted in him: "He knew a lot about medieval England, as I discovered when we visited Bodiam Castle together. . . . Ford's ideas, his way of looking at art and life, belong to a vanished world. In the catastrophe of chaos they have become meaningless." [5]

5. Richard Aldington, *Life for Life's Sake* (New York, 1941), p. 159.

Ford's concept of opposed north and south European mentality and culture plays an integral part in shaping the plot, character, and theme in *A Call*. First there is the contrast between passion and restraint; but more important is that implied contrast between the medieval, Catholic, and communalistic concept of an integrated society and a modern spirit that is individualistic, opportunistic, and dissidently Protestant. It is this latter contrast between the two civilizations that lies at the center of Ford's historical and ethnological assumptions, assumptions that grew steadily stronger toward the end of his life. *Great Trade Route*, as we have said, sets forth Ford's last and most complete statement of these ideas. This book, in defending the cultural values of the Mediterranean civilization against the predatory influence of the Nordic, is clearly Ford's final summing up, unfolding as it does his entire *apparat*:

> What is certain is that our civilization—I am not talking of our ability to evolve and make others work machines—our civilization was born of the Great Route and, in so far as our civilization has beauties and virtues it derives them from the Merchants and their pupils. You can put it that in so far as we are civilized beings—beings fitted to live the one beside the other without friction—it is because of the workings in our minds of that Chinese-Greek-Latin civilization's Mediterranean leaven. Where we Nordics are predatory, bloodthirsty, blind, reckless, and apt to go berserker, it is because we have in our veins the blood of peoples that, after or towards the end of the age of the Sacred Merchants, were born, multiplied, and over peopled the forests, swamps, and heaths to the north of the Great Route.[6]

Ford's explanation of why the Nordic mentality—despite its cold-fish temperament—was more apt to go "berserker" is that the north European's coldness is really a dangerous restraint, leading to eventual eruptions, whereas the Latinate personality channels potentially dangerous passions off into a healthy expression of day-to-day passions, sentiments, and feelings. Unquestionably Ford's best cameo description of these opposing temperaments appears in *Mr. Fleight*

6. *Great Trade Route*, p. 29.

in the characters of Blood and Fleight. Blood, the brooding, misan-
thropic Britisher, does indeed go "berserker," on one occasion stran-
gling a groom, while Fleight, a Jew of the Mediterranean culture, is
a meek and gentle alien, with healthy appetites and financial and
political success, gradually crowding the Nordic type off the stage.
The dilemma of Grimshaw in *A Call* is that as an Anglo-Greek
temperamental hybrid (hence his psychological conflict), it is his
misfortune to have been born at the tail end of that tradition of class
responsibility dating back to the middle ages; nor does he immediately perceive how this tradition has withered in the North, so that
his only really positive value is of no advantage to him here. Ironically it leads to his failure in a social milieu indifferent to his values
and temperament, Ford's usual formula for his alien protagonists.
Consequently Ford's concern in writing *A Call* was more deeply
aimed than those critics suggest who see it primarily as an attempt to
impress upon the readers and contributors of his *English Review* his
own ability as a writer. In it he sought to produce a work of fiction
that would fulfill the highest obligation of art as he proclaimed that
obligation a year later in *The Critical Attitude:* "The Province of
Art . . . is the bringing of humanity into contact, person with
person." [7] It was necessary, Ford argued, that art should show the
Englishman to himself as he really was. Grimshaw, as alien protagonist, was the satiric counter in which the English were to recognize
their own national deficiency. Later in the novel the despondent
protagonist is told by a Greek Orthodox priest, "One may perceive
that you are not English, for the English do not, like you, seek to
come into contact with their fellow beings . . ." (p. 220).

In the Latinate side of Grimshaw's psychology Ford had sought
to suggest to Englishmen what the British national spirit had lost in
its evolutionary estrangement from the values of the Mediterranean
and feudal frame of mind and that subsequent growth of individualism and dissidence under the aegis of Germanic protestantism. It is

7. Ford Madox Ford, *The Critical Attitude* (London, 1911), p. 30.

Grimshaw's estranged lover who analyzes for him the breakdown in communication and human relationships of the modern period—that favorite thesis Bloomsbury was to take over from its predecessors: " 'Ah,' she said slowly, and she looked at him with the straight, remorseless glance and spoke with the little, cold expressionless voice that made him think of her for the rest of his life as if she were the unpitying angel that barred for our first parents the return into Eden, 'you see that at last! That is where we all are—flying as far apart as the poles.' " (p. 273) In terms of a lost Golden Age, the Eden image has triple significance: it symbolizes the irretrievable loss of Grimshaw's cultural ideal and the more immediate loss of the woman he loves, and in a broader sense the loss of innocence itself. Self-knowledge has come to him, but, as with Ford's other protagonists, it comes too late to save him. Nothing is left but to bear the consequences of his meddling: loss of the woman he loves, marriage with another, and a bleak life in a society he had sought vainly to alter according to his own cultural ideals. The novel dramatically affirms that continuing breakdown in human relationships, that very breakdown the *English Review* had been founded in order to combat.

The *Review*, established to achieve the same high aims afterwards proclaimed in *The Critical Attitude*, shortly passed out of Ford's hands, its goals unaccomplished, though later writers, notably the Bloomsbury group, were to seek them after their own fashion. With Ford the quest had prompted a search for a protagonist whose struggle with his society would suggest implicity the deterioration of the British national character. Given the protean nature of the Edwardian temper, with no common terms of moral reference by which to judge the admirable from the unadmirable, Ford was driven to seek a protagonist from remote dimensions in time and space, a protagonist who represented a perfectly alien, though systematic standard of conduct and values. Ford discovered the formula in Katherine Howard and the moral-historical dilemma that provides the dramatic conflict of the Tudor novels, went on to develop it in Edward Colman of *The "Half-Moon,"* and began experimenting with it in a modern setting with protagonists like Don Kelleg and Robert Grimshaw—and later Fleight, Sorrell, Ashburnham, and Tietjens. Only the latter two are so perfectly realized, their satiric function so accommodated and subdued to impressionistic objectivity that the echoes of Ford's historical theories are but a low rumble on the horizons of the novels.

These are the personae from behind which Ford launched his criticism of the Edwardian cultural establishment. And it may be, as one critic has suggested, that Ford's own mixed personality played at least an unconscious part in arriving at the technique.[8] Be this as it may, all of Ford's early protagonists represent ethical "outsiders," historical or ethnographical, incapable of operating in the present and therefore ruthlessly set aside in favor of more normative types. With Grimshaw of *A Call* one notes the barest alteration in the technique. Less crudely extracted from an earlier historical epoch, he nonetheless, by dint of his Latinate blood, represents a "foreign" culture that has preserved intact a social order dating back to the medieval period, an order lost to those Nordic nations where the dislocations of industrialism have maimed the modern spirit, destroying those human contacts championed by English humanists from the mid-nineteenth century on.

Despite the ethnographic turn Ford's technique was taking, the nature and resolution of dramatic conflict in the novels remains unchanged: ultimately the alien protagonist fails; but that failure still signals the deficiences of a modern society blind to the traditional values of its own past. And in that fated failure and blindness Ford was at last achieving the sense of inevitability he and Conrad held to be the cornerstone of their mutual art and of that destiny, blind and inscrutable, in which they both believed:

Before everything a story must convey a sense of inevitability: that which happens in it must seem to be the only thing that could have hap-

8. R. W. Lid, "Return to Yesterday," *Jubilee*, IX (March, 1962), 38.

pened. . . . The problem of the author is to make this then action the only action that character could have taken. It must be inevitable, because of his character, because of his ancestry . . . or on account of the gradual coming together of the thousand small circumstances by which Destiny, who is inscrutable and august, will push us into one certain predicament.[9]

Before the creation of the Ashburnham figures in *The Good Soldier,* that perfect summation of the medievalist in modern dress, Ford was to write two more novels, each representing significant variations upon his alien protagonist. The first of these, *Ladies Whose Bright Eyes,* was published the year after *A Call;* the second, *Mr. Fleight,* appeared two years later in 1913. In both novels the alien protagonist appears and his function remains that of the moral yardstick by which one may measure the modern decline. In *Ladies Whose Bright Eyes* there is a partial reversion to Ford's historical system and the dramatic conflict arising from the old psychological cyclicalism as Ford sought for the first time a direct confrontation of modern and medieval world views. Unsatisfied with his previous attempts to exemplify the medieval spirit in terms of a single, vestigial figure, he turned instead to a panoramic view of the medieval scene itself, altered his old technique, and made his cultural outsider a citizen of the twentieth century whose representative qualities posed less of a problem for the modern reader than his earlier attempts to evoke sympathy for an isolated medieval figure out of a remote and unfamiliar past. *Mr. Fleight,* on the other hand, reflects Ford's growing emphasis upon popular ethnology as a basis for contrasting human racial psychologies and cultural ideals, both drawn from existing societies. The temperamental clash of the Nordic and Latinate spirit in *A Call* develops into a quite open implementation of racial theories then current in Edwardian England: those half-thought-out assumptions of de Gobineau, Houston Chamberlain, and de Lapouge as well as the whole dreary rout of Wagnerites and pan-Germanists active in these years.

Mr. Sorrell of *Ladies Whose Bright Eyes,* an enthusiastic mod-

9. Ford Madox Ford, *Joseph Conrad: A Personal Remembrance* (New York, 1965), p. 245.

ernist, is transported back in time to the England of Edward III, the result of a head injury received in a railway accident. A fantasy device borrowed from Mark Twain, it was also an attempt to exploit the popularity of Wellsian time-travellers, itself an outgrowth of that brief flurry of interest in the fourth dimension at the Royal College of Science during the late 1880s. In this novel Ford reverses the role previously played by the alien protagonist. Formerly an outdated relic from an earlier time slot, the protagonist of *Ladies Whose Bright Eyes*, Sorrell, represents the modern psychological dominant type suddenly thrown back into the earlier and unfamiliar environment of the middle ages. The peculiar and specialized talents that made him dominant on the modern scene are useless to him in the medieval world, and his standards of values and human behavior are inappropriate to the demands of the medieval Time Spirit. The shrewd, cautious, and sedentary product of the future, he is no match for the energetic and choleric medieval characters, male and female, who surround him on Salisbury Plain in the mid-fourteenth century. The most enthusiastically reviewed of any of Ford's novels at the time, *Ladies Whose Bright Eyes* has gained scant credit with critics today, who often prefer the revised edition of 1935 where, it is argued, the resolution of Sorrell's problem is more realistically handled—a specious argument inasmuch as Sorrell comes quite solidly to terms with the divergent demands of both medieval and modern world, a quandary earlier protagonists have been unable to resolve. Other critics argue the novel stems from Ford's pique over Twain's misrepresentation of the medieval scene. While defending Rossetti against willful anachronism in depicting his medieval subjects, Ford had complained of "Mark Twain's *Yankee at the Court of King Arthur* [*sic*], where dummy knights in armour are discomfitted by electrified barbed wire, and a modern American perturbs King Arthur by preaching down chivalric ideals to the tune of nineteenth century morality." [10] Though Ford's qualified admiration

10. Ford Madox Ford, *Rossetti: A Critical Essay on His Art* (London, 1914), p. 49.

of the middle ages is apparent in scenes depicting courtyards strewn with offal, egg shells, and rotting carcasses, it is undeniably the work of the artist raised in the Pre-Raphaelite hothouse of medieval culture. And though Ford would personally have agreed with Walter Bagehot, who once wrote that "all sensible people know that the middle ages must have been very uncomfortable," *Ladies Whose Bright Eyes* unfolds as an incredibly rich and detailed Pre-Raphaelite painting. In fact a number of the battlement scenes appear to have taken their inspiration from Burne-Jones's paintings, particularly his *Going to the Battle*, inspired by both Rossetti's "Froissartian" water colors and Dürer's castle architecture.

Where Twain riveted attention on the barbarism of the medieval period and through omission and tone falsified its positive side, Ford answered with a more realistic appraisal of the age, suggesting at the same time the relative inadequacies of the modern world in the person of William Sorrell, the representative twentieth-century man. It is with Sorrell, with his modern physiognomy and Nordic stock, that the novel opens: "Mr. Sorrell was accustomed to regard himself as a typical representative of the Homo-Sapiens Europaeus. He was rising forty; he was rather fair with fresh, brown hair; he had a drooping brown mustache and a pink, clear skin." The fair hair and pink skin immediately betray Sorrell as a foreigner to the medieval world, especially when one recalls the brown and weatherbeaten hues and dark hair coloring Ford consistently attributed to the medieval types of the historical novels and uses with the fourteenth-century characters in this novel. By contrast Ford's modern figures—the representative ones—are always fair-haired and pink-skinned, characters like Augusta Macphail or the Baroness di Sonnino of *Mr. Fleight* or Lady Aldington of *The New Humpty-Dumpty*. Sorrell and his pink-faced brethren represent the Protestant and Germanic stock directly descended from that of the Cinque Ports Dutchmen of *The "Half-Moon."* The dominant psychological type representing the Time Spirit of that age is continually opposed, by values and temperament, to Ford's dark-haired and swarthy medieval throwbacks or those modern Mediterranean types all poured from the same mold—figures like Norfolk, Anne Jeal, Count Canzano, Henry Hudson, Robert Grimshaw, Mr. Fleight, or the Lady Blanche of this novel, whose "weather-beaten and coloured beauty appear dusky and negligible" by contrast with Sorrell, the pink-skinned interloper from the twentieth century.

This modern type, winding down to extinction in Ford's mind, is characterized by physical weakness on the one hand and that murderous Nordic imperial mentality on the other. Ready to set about exploiting these apparently ignorant medievalists through his modern knowledge of gunpowder and airplanes, Sorrell comes eventually to the shamefaced realization that he has no real knowledge of how to produce either one. By contrast, the powerful and lusty Lady Blanche, wielding her enormous two-handed sword, makes short work of Sorrell's captors and takes him captive for her own uses. And her own sexual aggressiveness contrasts strongly with his sexual diffidence displayed in the introductory pages of the novel. In that progressive curbing of man's passions in favor of social prudence the modern world has become flat, stale, and unprofitable. Even Lady Blanche's day, Ford suggests, represents something of a falling off from the real heyday of medievalism: "She [Lady Blanche] would have loved to use force, which was more in her character than any kind of guile. . . . In the hardier old times of which she had heard her grandfather and father speak, and to which she felt herself to belong—in those times she would calmly have killed the bearer of the cross and have hidden the cross itself in the stones of the wall of her bower. . . ." (p. 119)

This is that same atavistic longing displayed by Norfolk, who, frustrated by Tudor guile, cannot understand his archbishop's reluctance to wrack and burn for the faith, or Katherine Howard, who, in a rage, can beat a serving man about the head with the fireplace tongs. Sorrell, who stands for man five hundred years farther down the evolutionary path, reflects that "national . . . spirit already on the wane" that Ford had described in *England and the English*. But

Sorrell, unlike so many of Ford's cultural misfits, recovers—largely because he absorbs something of the medieval spirit, thus realizing those latent human powers that have lain dormant in this dominant type since the growth of Dutch-Protestant commercialism. When Sorrell first awakens to find himself in the time of Edward III he is still characterized by the physical disabilities and mental insularity Ford ascribes to his Edwardian contemporaries in *The Critical Attitude,* which he was writing at the same moment. Though a publisher, Sorrell is deeply ignorant of history and has nothing but contempt for imaginative fiction: "I don't believe in novels and nonsense of that sort, unless I can be absolutely certain they'll have a large sale." By the end of the novel Sorrell has become physically active and shows a healthy interest in both fiction and history.

But before he can be reclaimed totally, Sorrell must come to terms with the entire spectrum of values represented by Ford's brand of medievalism. One of those typically fragmented moderns he is initially ill at ease in the tightly knit, economically interdependent communalism of the medieval world. And his religious indifferentism comes hard up against medieval Catholicism with its more rigorous judgment of matters both lay and clerical. In Sorrell's Edwardian world religious conviction has dwindled into the fraudulent table-rapping of Madame Blavatsky—like cranks and charlatans:

> Mr. Sorrell had never taken much interest in spiritualism and that sort of thing. . . . But you could not help knocking against it. There was the drawing room of his aunt, Old Lady Wells, to which he went occasionally . . . on a Sunday afternoon, and it was always full of estimable people, who told him the most extraordinary things, that you could not in the ordinary way believe in. He had heard of the dead speaking from a distance, just as he had heard of the stone-blind being cured by Christian Science, the new Homeopathy or by mere psychic force. [p. 83]

There is less sense of fateful determinism hanging over *Ladies Whose Bright Eyes* than in previous novels and by its conclusion Ford suggests the possibility of recovery, though this involves, as one would expect, a partial return to medieval modes and manners.

In many respects Sorrell is that stock figure of Edwardian fiction: a study in self-discovery like Strether or Mr. Polly. Close to that fatal languor of middle life, he is saved by lucky chance and forced into the exercise of latent abilities, by which both life and personality are changed. In the course of the novel the protagonist undergoes steady alteration, becoming increasingly the medieval man of violence and action. And though this alteration is awkwardly handled —coming as it does in fits and starts—Sorrell by the end has become a much more satisfying character.

Returned to the modern scene, Sorrell sets about learning history, publishing poetry, and reconstructing a ruined medieval castle, doing much of the physical labor with his own hands. But before this somewhat unbelievable transformation, he obviously represents a recognizable variation on Ford's alien protagonist, the man somehow out of step with the times in which he finds himself. Here however, thanks to Twain in part, the reader is made explicitly aware that he is seeing a contrast of historical epochs. And unlike the earlier avatars of this type, Sorrell is an obvious break with the hero of principles and ideals struggling against an immoral or amoral Time Spirit, just as the novel as a whole is an attempt to throw the respective values of the medieval and modern into starker relief through immediate confrontation. Social criticism here is directed not at the milieu against which the isolated protagonist struggles but against that from which he has come and of which he is the dramatic embodiment. So although the satiric vehicle is still the alien protagonist, the reader's sympathies are less centered in him. It is Gulliver amongst the Houyhnhnms again. That which becomes suspect is the point of view of the protagonist himself as he looks out uncomprehendingly across the medieval landscape, a technique anticipating that of *The Good Solider*. In that later novel it is the eye of Dowell, the shrunken effigy of modern man, that provides the lens through which the reader follows the medievalist Ashburnham as he fumbles his way into failure and death in a hostile world order.

Still *Ladies Whose Bright Eyes* is but a partial success, for much the same reason *The Inheritors* and *Mr. Apollo* had been failures. It is less the element of fantasy than the tone Ford adopts for this dream vision of the past that weakens both the impressionistic rendering of the medieval scenes and those criticisms of contemporary life built into it. Though the book is not restricted to Sorrell's point of view, his is primarily the perspective from which we view the medieval world. The fragile shell of the reader's suspended disbelief is shattered repeatedly by Sorrell's constant reminder that all is a momentary audio-visual hallucination quite apt to disappear with another rap on the head. In addition there is that continual jarring disparity between the often somber, and in themselves convincing, Pre-Raphaelite scenes and the protagonist's broadly vernacular commentary upon those scenes. At one point in his adventures Sorrell encounters a man whose visual resemblance to a modern acquaintance tells him he is looking at the fellow's remote ancestor: "I suppose that wretched little bad hat would be the descendant of this old knight who went walloping dragons round Cairo way." Though Kenneth Young admires these tonal variations as "displays of a most delicious gift of the comic," [11] they seem to belie Ford's seriousness with respect to the novel's social criticism, an endemic weakness in Ford's work which was once pointed out to him by his American publisher: "Hueffer, the Americans will never read you because they cannot tell whether you are in earnest or not and the English will not because you are too damn in earnest." [12]

Equally serious as the failure of tone is Ford's lapse from those canons of objectivity he never ceased to expound; and the closing scene of *Ladies Whose Bright Eyes* concludes with a rather dreary and undramatic exchange of ideas in the Shavian manner. Given the burden of the novel's historical "message," it is understandable that so many of Ford's early novels—inaccurately described as "renderings" by Ford himself—should have had recourse to some closing

11. Kenneth Young, *Ford Madox Ford* (New York and Toronto, 1956), p. 25.

12. Ford Madox Ford, *Return to Yesterday* (New York, 1932), p. 336.

scene with a more or less open commentary on the implications of the actions and events of the novel, implications Ford had not been able to suggest implicitly in action and dialogue. Not even *The Good Soldier* was to escape this completely. In place of the gradual revelation of character so handsomely managed in *A Call*, Ford lapsed into the manner of his favorite villains, the Victorian novelists: the omniscient author, resorting to first-person commentary at one point in the novel. And the mordant humor of the critical and social commentary is so clearly the Ford of the reminiscences that all attempt at the detached narrative voice is lost as Ford becomes the medieval raconteur, telling that "straightfoward tale in straightforward language" for which he ridiculed the Victorians.[13]

But perhaps most puzzling of all these apparent regressions is the structural motley comprising the book, for the novel is an amalgam of variant techniques and narrative actions. It is by turns dream fantasy, social satire, historical romance, medieval travelogue, at times even farce. And if this were not enough, the entire central portion of the book has nothing to do with the opening and closing sections. These scenes, set not on Salisbury Plain but in the Scots border country, are totally divorced in character, setting, and action from the remainder of the novel. Here the historical events are drawn from the sections of Froissart's *Chronicles* describing the falling out between the followers of John of Hainault and the supporters of the young Edward III and his mother, the Queen-regent of those years. It was a small skirmish but one that summed up the Englishman's brooding resentment of Queen Isabella's employment of French troops to overthrow and later murder her husband Edward III. Ford's treatment of these incidents is completely unlike his handling of the material involving Sorrell, with his subsequent adventures in the shadow of Salisbury Cathedral many miles to the south. In the northern scenes Ford uses all the Impressionist's devices so palpably absent from the remainder of the novel—the restricted

13. *Ibid.*, p. 214.

and intensified focus built around two knights, Egerton and de Coucy, who fight the good fight in behalf of their slain monarch.

Ford's approach in this central section is "scenic" rather than "panoramic," depending on dialogue and interior monologue rather than third-person exposition. And there is a level of sustained high seriousness in these chapters quite unlike the remainder of the novel, which often pokes gratuitous fun at itself. Consequently there is a strong suggestion of interpolation in these parts—a suggestion that Ford simply inserted a body of material, which had been originally intended for fuller treatment elsewhere, with the seams but crudely smoothed over. As far as its significance for the main action of the novel is concerned, the entire central portion could have been, and more logically should have been, handled in a page or two.

What invites speculation about these extraneous scenes is their marked resemblance to Ford's habitual situation involving the alien protagonist, that fated entanglement between personal values and historical process in which the representative of the past inevitably fails in the face of the new *Zeitgeist*. De Coucy and Egerton, perfect medieval types in their slow-witted violence and idealism, maintain their chivalric and slightly quixotic loyalty to their murdered monarch, Edward III. Their antagonists, followers of Queen Isabella, are neither idealistic nor hardy, preferring to overcome by guile and duplicity after the manner of the Tudor Machiavellian in the Katherine Howard trilogy. And the lines of conflict are equally characteristic—the struggle of passion and altruism against new forces rising on the historical scene—but these conflicts relate only tangentially to the remainder of the novel. Nor is this brilliant episode in any way linked to the larger satiric aims of the novel, which are completely concentrated in the events taking place on Salisbury Plain. In fact, with the shift to the northern scenes, all remembrance of the twentieth century fades out and the medieval-modern satiric contrast gives way to the historical impressionism of the Katherine Howard novels. This promising fragment comes to nothing and the reason for its inclusion remains an unsolved riddle.

Later in life Ford was to recall these financially difficult years as ones in which he had written "extremely bad novels at a very great speed."[14] A crude vehicle for Ford's medieval idealism, *Ladies Whose Bright Eyes* is his least illustrious achievement in which the alien protagonist figures at all prominently. Depending on the sensationalistic, without the redeeming scientific imagination of Wells, Ford had sought a quick and easy device of contrasting the medieval and modern world. Abandoning the old clash of successive psychological types thrown together in periods of historical transition, such as he had portrayed in the Tudor novels and in *The "Half-Moon,"* Ford resorted to an alien protagonist who, through the device of dream fantasy moves back in time to an unfamiliar cultural setting. Subsequently Ford was able to describe first hand the world that previously his reader had been forced to reconstruct mentally from the actions and words of a Katherine Howard. And though *Ladies Whose Bright Eyes* is an undoubted reaffirmation of Ford's qualified admiration for the medieval world, the novel shows him still uncertain how to incorporate the values of that world in a meaningful contrast with the twentieth-century spirit, such as he had been working toward in the ethnological approach of *A Call*. And it was to this approach he would return in *Mr. Fleight,* published two years after *Ladies Whose Bright Eyes.*

"Politics in a work of literature," wrote Stendhal, "is like a pistol-shot in the middle of a concert, something loud and vulgar, and yet a thing to which it is not possible to refuse one's attention." Without being either loud or vulgar, Ford's *Mr. Fleight* (1913) attracted the attention noted by Stendhal, if judged by the enthusiastic reviews and general reception. A reviewer in *Outlook* called it a "slight epic in satire. . . . A brilliant, distinguished, memorable book."[15] The majority of reviewers applauded the humor of Ford's satire, though they were disappointed with the thinness of its political analysis and the peculiarity of one of its main characters, Mr.

14. *Ibid.,* p. 392.
15. Review of *Mr. Fleight, Outlook,* XXXI (May 24, 1913), 722.

Blood. But this was to miss the point completely for the book is not essentially a political novel any more than *The Secret Agent* is, and it can only suffer in being categorized as one. As for the "peculiarity" of Mr. Blood, he can only seem so to one totally ignorant of Ford's historical system or unmindful of popular Edwardian notions of ethnology. Quite rightfully such concerns are not the responsibility of the reader, and the fact that Ford has failed to make these things apparent within the novel testifies to his continuing difficulty in making his *sub rosa* concepts of historical change dramatically plausible and convincing in terms of action and characterization.

As a study of the Edwardian political scene the novel is inconsequential, but the political setting has only peripheral relevance for the novel's real worth as an ethnological analysis of Edwardian society seen against a concept of social and psychological evolution reaching both forward and backward in time. The politics of the novel are only the occasion for an examination of the deeper social and cultural deterioration underlying the entire Edwardian era, a deterioration linked in Ford's historical system to the increasing credence given the continental racial theories of writers like de Gobineau and de Lapouge, trumpeted by pan-Germanists across the land.

Modern criticism, largely unaware of Ford's historicism, has arrived at no common consensus about *Mr. Fleight*, either of its tenor or its place in Ford's artistic development. Cassell says it shows "the not altogether admirable encroachment of the monied Jew into British politics." [16] Paul Wiley, more perceptively, calls the novel Ford's most ambitious and successful before *The Good Soldier*, "a cardinal example of Ford's Impressionist aim to reduce potential Zolaesque breadth to the restricted focus of an Affair. . . ." [17] Certainly the vibrations of the affair here reach out into a myriad of social levels almost Dickensian and in a manner far more ambitious than Ford's previous probings of the contemporary scene.

16. Richard A. Cassell, *Ford Madox Ford: A Study of His Novels* (Baltimore, 1961), p. 137.
17. *Novelist of Three Worlds*, p. 164.

As for any "peculiarity" in the conception of the novel's two main characters, they are precisely what Ford intended them to be. Again it is Paul Wiley who has seen most closely what Ford was up to in his suggestion that somehow the contrast between Mr. Blood and Mr. Fleight is intended to suggest the reason for the collapse of aristocratic conventions during the post-Victorian breakup. As a matter of fact, this is *precisely* what does lie behind the conception of these two characters, each of whom is a near allegorical representation of his respective Time Spirit, as well as the ethnic group from which he has sprung. Each of those three successive periods in Ford's grand scheme of things—the medieval, the Tudor-Stuart, and the modern—saw the ascendancy of a different ethnic group from which "the leading spirits," as Ford called them, would emerge. For the medieval period this had been the old "French-Norman" stock, for the Tudor-Stuart the "Italian-Celtic," while the modern period came as a result of "a calling out of the Germanic forces of the nation." [18]

Even as he was writing, Ford perceived that Demos in his stirring, as Bennett suspected, was ushering in still another dominant type to replace that which had persisted since the days of William of Orange: "We imagine perhaps a change in the national psychology. And I am quite prepared to have it said that these pages—if they get any spirit at all—get only at a national spirit that is already on the wane." [19] *Mr. Fleight* is an attempt to describe not simply the waning of the old, but the direction and the very ethnic group from which would arise the new World Individual who would guide England through the coming generations, "the father of the age to come," as one character in the novel puts it. As in those earlier shifts between dominant types there would come a wholesale revolution in the psychological makeup of the new wave, as well as the usual distinctive physiological and physiognomic alterations.

Misunderstanding Ford's view of the Jew as an alien cultural force

18. Ford, *England and the English*, pp. 283–84.
19. *Ibid.*, p. 354.

about to rejuvenate English stock, one critic has leveled the dreary charge of anti-Semitism against Ford for his handling of the Jewish Fleight. Meixner quotes a number of vaguely anti-Semitic passages out of other contexts, arguing that Mr. Fleight presents a "similar attitude of anti-Semitic class superiority. . . ." [20] Such determined misreading drives Meixner paradoxically to explain how it is that Fleight turns out the most exemplary character in the novel: "the most attractive and the most sympathetic character in the book," as he himself admits. [21] Whatever there may have been of anti-Semitism in Ford's make-up, there is no basis for such a charge in *Mr. Fleight*. If anything, there is rather the obvious suggestion of ethical and moral superiority in Fleight, a superiority that sets him apart from the less admirable light-skinned, Anglo-Saxon figures around him. These figures recognize his natural superiority and in that recognition set about exploiting his ethnic uniqueness.

Much of the critical confusion and uncertainty surrounding *Mr. Fleight* stems from the failure of critics to discern the ethnological assumptions underlying the social conflicts dramatized in the novel, and the relationship of those assumptions to Ford's concept of historical cycles of growth, stasis, and decline. This decline is reflected largely through the political material in the novel; and though there is little originality in Ford's generalized notions of racial phenomena and cultural breakdown, no other English novelist of his day has made such wholesale use of these commonplaces of the Edwardian intellectual market place. Although this is not to suggest that the novel is solely a vehicle for current racial theory, these theories are obviously of more concern to Ford than any fleeting political issues, thereby mitigating the charge that the novel fails as political satire by reducing the political aspects of the novel to their proper perspective.

Influenced perhaps by the success of Wells's *The New Machia-*

20. John A. Meixner, *Ford Madox Ford's Novels* (Minneapolis, 1962), p. 111.
21. *Ibid.*

*velli, Mr. Fleight* signals a return to the general theme of *The Inheritors*, the early collaboration with Conrad published in 1901. In both novels there is the tendency to interpret political opportunism and pragmatism as a symptom of general cultural collapse. In the earlier novel the *ancien régime*, with its aristocratic notions of honor and integrity, is about to be displaced by an improbable invasion of other dimensional beings, unprincipled and pragmatic, as they scheme to discredit the existing government before their take-over. It was, as we have seen, an allegorical representation of the new and strident voices, Richard Remington's among them, of the new imperial temper which seemed to threaten the entire fabric of British civilization and to hint at some disastrous turn in the English national spirit.[22]

In *Mr. Fleight* Ford, by now fourteen novels wiser, avoided the sort of allegorical fantasy that weakened the sense of social concern in the earlier novel. Instead of attributing the changing mood of English spirit and politics to an invasion of alien beings from the Fourth Dimension, Ford turned to his historical analysis of English history, with its assumption of altering psychological types based on differing racial stocks. And yet there is the thinnest thread of connection between the early novel and this. *Mr. Fleight* deals openly with the impact of the Jew on English politics, but even in the earlier novel Granger, the young protagonist, had suggested the ethnic origin of the strange young female Dimensionist he has met: "She must be of some race, perhaps Semitic . . . of some incompatible race." Tenuous as the link is, it does suggest Ford's continual search for an alien cultural alternative lying outside of northern Europe. Where there is little to admire in the new political dynamic of *The Inheritors*, there is much that is admirable in the character of Fleight, who represents the usurping political force in the later novel.

22. See especially Ford Madox Ford, *Memories and Impressions* (New York, 1911), p. 171.

If as Irving Howe has suggested the political novel is "a novel in which political ideas play a dominant role," then *Mr. Fleight* is assuredly no such thing, for it touches on none of the three major political issues of the Edwardian period: the suffragette movement, the working man's revolt, or the Irish question. Ford, as he has noted in many of his reminiscences, is really indifferent to these questions [23] and is content to tilt at those tired old whipping boys: jobbery, nepotism, and demagogy in this generalized chronicle of a demoralized society. Surprisingly enough Ford succeeded wonderfully in capturing the flavor of the period, which as an Impressionist was his goal. Edgar Jepson in his *Memoirs of an Edwardian* calls it "the best presentation of polite and cultured London at the end of the Edwardian Age." [24] And Amy Cruse in *After the Victorians* lists it as a staple in the reading of any socially conscious Edwardian. [25]

Unlike Jane Austen, who had the advantage of a relatively stable society from which to present her sociohistorical profiles, Ford could assume no substrata of shared beliefs in the prolixity that comprised the Edwardian era. And so as an Impressionist whose responsibility was to render the immediate scene Ford sought instinctively for those settings that best registered the protean spirit of the times. Into the turbulence of conflicting ideas and uncertain conventions Ford sent his alien protagonists, men not unlike those of Stendhal, heroic individuals no longer able to hold out in an age of mass ideology—such as threatens the private and ethical worlds of men like Fleight, Ashburnham, and Tietjens.

A wholesale assault on all Ford thought reprehensible in the post–Boer War world, the novel drew bead on the day's political mediocrity and the self-serving literary periodicals that wafted the

23. See Ford's repeated statements of his interested but uninvolved awareness of the political events of his day in *Return to Yesterday* (especially chap. ii) and Ford Madox Ford, *A Mirror to France* (New York, 1926), p. 111.
24. Edgar Jepson, *Memories of an Edwardian and Neo-Georgian* (London, 1937), p. 134.
25. Amy Cruse, *After the Victorians* (London, 1938), pp. 202–4.

tired clichés of the politicians abroad. The exhausted attitudinizing of Soho intellectual bohemians as well as the mentally impoverished working classes—all find themselves satirized within the novel. Ford's social criticism here is self-evident, but from what point of view could these things be seen as enormities? In short, how does the reader get his bearings in order to form a comparative judgment of this Mad Hatter's party [26] where anything goes? Ford manages his satirical contrast principally through the figure of Fleight, an alien temperament who embodies a standard of values unlike either of the contending forces one initially meets in the novel. On the one hand there is Parment, the prime minister, an aging Liberal mystigogue given to vague and oracular utterances on the "necessity of idealism," thereby "making a formidable bid, in a demogogic manner, for the dictatorship of the country" (p. 49). Parment exemplifies a type of statecraft that Ford had observed growing since the eighties and that stretched, he argued elsewhere, from Gladstone to Lloyd George:

The privileged classes . . . were no doubt right in hating him [Gladstone]. A renegade from their ranks [Ford makes Parment a refugee from the Conservative party], he, more than any man, knew the weak places in their armour. With each successive ministry he became more and more destructive to them. . . . The Liberal Prime Ministers who followed him were almost all pale replicas of his figure. . . . They had of course personalities of their own. Lord Rosebery was a jocular and sporting peer . . . Mr. George the most sanguine of small country attorneys and the most impassioned of special pleaders. But, be their voices what they might, their plow hands were the hands of Gladstone. It was his furrow that they prolonged.[27]

In his oracular mystigoguery Parment less resembles Gladstone than he does Lloyd George, a perfect example of the Nordic mind gone mad and mystical. Ford's Parment is unmistakably Lloyd George as Maurois recalls him: "He was compared to the wizards of Nordic

26. For Ford's interesting use of the Mad Hatter image in connection with British politics, see *Mr. Fleight* (London, 1913), pp. 276 ff.
27. *Return to Yesterday*, pp. 94–95.

folklore. He had their powers of enchantment . . . their fatal and formidable gift of poetry . . . which makes the orator say what he hardly knows he is saying, and excites his listeners without their knowing why they are excited." [28]

Ford hopefully believed that by the close of the Edwardian period this type of dominant figure had come to the end of its historical cycle. For this reason Parment is presented in the novel as a vestigial remnant, a historical survival from an earlier period doomed now to extinction, as the astute Blood points out: "The Chancellor's old-fashioned with his enthusiasms. . . . Perfectly honest and perfectly decent, but quite hopeless. A doomed type." (p. 84) Whenever one comes upon Ford's phrase "doomed type," it is fairly certain that Ford's concept of historical and evolutionary determinism is lying someplace in the immediate background. The novel really abounds in outdated historical types which have anachronistically survived into the present. And the one who antedates even the Chancellor is Mr. Blood. A Huxley-like character, Blood in his revulsion at the mendacious spectacle of the modern world has withdrawn from active political life and made a shrine of his own nausea, linking him to figures like Greville in *An English Girl* and Mark Tietjens of *The Last Post*. An anachronistic survival from an earlier historical epoch, he gazes with Nietzschean arrogance at the modern scene before him: "Mr. Blood was a singular and mysterious person to such of his world as had observed his existence. A hundred years ago he would have represented the Englishman and gentleman. . . . In that age Mr. Blood would have been the commonest thing of his class and station. . . . He was, in fact, just an anachronism and an inactive one at that." (p. 8)

In his disgust at Edwardian society, Blood conceives it as a colossal and bitter joke to back the political career of Aaron Rothweil Fleight, a figure emblematic of those Rand millionaires who Ford felt had been firmly entrenched in Mayfair as a result of the South

28. André Maurois, *The Edwardian Era* (New York, 1933), p. 261.

African war.[29] Blood, disapproving of the irresponsible liberalism of the Gladstonian heritage, is equally cynical in his decision to promote the career of Fleight. Though he recognizes that the times are ripe for one of Fleight's mercantile background, he has only an inkling of the vaster Ford universe that makes men like Fleight the wave of the future. Approached too systematically, the motivations of Blood inevitably yield contradictions. At one point Blood's entire motive in supporting Fleight is simply a Nietzschean impulse to manipulate human affairs, though at other times it seems a calculated effort by a decadent privileged class to perpetuate its historical advantages. At these moments Blood does evidence a personal strategy for outwitting the idealistic demagogues who run the country as well as the rising Rand millionaires, a strategy not unlike the *espagnolism* exalted by Stendhal as a weapon against the politics of mass ideology.

The entire allegorical axis of the novel hinges on the two figures of Blood and Fleight, who re-enact on the modern scene the unending struggle between progress and tradition that typifies much of Ford's early work. Their names, as meaningful as those in the old morality plays, suggest the immediate quality of their characters. Blood, as his surname suggests, is a throwback to an earlier period; as an early critic said, his name suggests at once "both traditional aristocracy and a repressed inclination to bloodshed." [30] It was a type that Ford, for a time, felt might be coming into its own again and he wrote in *Memories and Impressions:* "It is a quaint thought, but a perfectly sound one, to say that we are nearer to habits of barbarism, that we could more easily revert to days of savagery than we could pick up again the tone of thought, of mind and habit, of the men of thirty years ago." [31] But in the context of the novel, at least, Blood represents a nearly extinct type, one that can exist but only under constraint. By nature compulsive and turbulent, he has once brutally

29. Ford, *Memories and Impressions*, p. 260.
30. Wiley, *Novelist of Three Worlds*, p. 166.
31. *Memories and Impressions*, p. 298.

strangled a groom for mistreating a horse, and discovers to his chagrin that this is still insufficient to provoke a direct retaliation from a febrile modernity, nor even ruffle its quiet and well-bred insouciance. Recognizing his impotence to operate in such a social context, he withdraws into brooding seclusion, content to watch from his club window the encroachment of the motor car upon the carriage traffic of an earlier era. It is here, in the opening scene, that he is discovered by Aaron Rothweil Fleight, the millionaire Jew with a moral compulsion to serve his adopted country. The physical contrast between the two is the visual symbol of England Past and England Future looking out on English Present: "A little dark man approached Mr. Blood, who sat in a deep armchair of the What Not Club. Mr. Blood, a heavy, grey man of ferocious aspect, was surveying the Thames. . . ." (p. 1)

The suggestion of ferocity, bulk, and grayness immediately recalls the opening description of Henry VIII in *The Fifth Queen*, and is the same psychophysiological type as Lord Aldington of *The New Humpty Dumpty*. Blood represents a type obviously out of place in the present. And though he does not function here as alien protagonist, he clearly identifies his dilemma as one of history's misplaced: "The only thing of my kind left in the world. Like the last mastodon." But the other half of this equation, the "little dark man," is equally alien to Edwardian society; only he, as Blood recognizes, is the wave of the future, the new dominant type. The coming dominion of this physiological type and its displacement of those like Blood Ford prophesied as early as *England and the English*: "There is an east of London population which is small, dark, vigorous and gentle. In the natural course of things this eastern population will rise in the scale, will cross London, will besiege the palaces. . . . We cannot nowadays say of what race are either the giants [like Blood] or the small dark men [like Fleight], still less will the sociologist of the future be able to pronounce upon what the origins of that mixed dominant race shall be." [32]

32. *England and the English*, p. 264.

The inevitability of that phrase "in the natural course of things" suggests that Ford may have taken his historical system more seriously than even he was aware when he called it "merely a convenient system of thought." Certainly Fleight represents one more ripple in those "waving lines" representing the rise and fall of variant types within Ford's cyclical process. Blood, recognizing his inevitable replacement by this new variation of the species, would prolong the tenure of the old feudal-aristocratic privilege as long as possible, by exploiting the success of the new type. Blood's younger brother, Reginald, explains this characteristic process in the political evolution of Western society: "The appearance of the Jew in our society means that the Jew is an unrivalled soldier of fortune. He isn't part of our country; he hasn't got our morality, but he's extraordinarily able as a ruler. So our side takes him up and uses him." (p. 213) The alien protagonist here, in addition to providing a corrective lens through which to view contemporary decadence, illustrates again that process of social selection that served Ford as a blueprint of historical conflict in the Katherine Howard novels. As early as 1907, in *England and the English*, Ford had spelled out in detail the process Reginald Blood described above: "The man among us, seeing his opportunity, will eventually burst through, and, being quick to follow a lead, we shall acclaim him, learn from him, reward him, let him and his tradition become an incubus on us in face of some rising age. . . ." [33] The statement is a perfect capsule commentary of narrative events in the novel, with Fleight representing the individual embodiment of the coming Time Spirit, as surely as Cromwell represented that of the sixteenth and early seventeenth centuries in the Tudor novels. The success of *Mr. Fleight* testifies to Ford's increasing sureness in dramatizing the struggles and antagonisms of history through characters who, in their deterministic psychologies, exemplify the larger pattern of social and historical forces. As his alien protagonist became an increasingly effective device of implicit criticism by which modern dissolution might be

33. *Ibid.*, p. 279.

measured, Ford had less often to resort to those crude explanatory scenes that exist as blemishes in early novels like *An English Girl*, *A Call*, and *Ladies Whose Bright Eyes*.

But there are other differences in the novel as well. For once Ford's alien protagonist succeeds and he does so because he represents the new Time Spirit descending upon England, "the child of the age," as Blood calls him. What is it in Fleight's psychology that makes him the appropriate vehicle for the Time Spirit of the late Edwardian age? It is his "small shopkeeper mentality," as both he and Blood term it. Blood, of course, uses the term contemptuously, though in Ford's scheme of things it counts for far more. Fleight's "mentality" or psychology is the ethical heritage of his Mediterranean stock, a stock that had grown up along "the Route of the Sacred Merchants," as Ford described it in *Great Trade Route*, nearly a quarter of a century later. Fleight, exhausted by the rigors of campaigning, tells a group of lower-class friends and constituents: "I've told you often enough that I'd rather sit here on a Saturday night when trade's busy than almost anywhere else in the world. . . . Unless it were sitting under an arch in a hot country selling Damascus silks, crosslegged." (p. 108) It was this way of life, the small merchant culture of the Mediterranean world, which Ford repeatedly insisted was the only salvation for a declining northern Europe, with its stultifying technocracy and monolithic combines run by predatory Nordics in a Darwinian commercial jungle. It was the "Sino-Helleno-Latin civilization of the Mediterranean," the home of the "Sacred Merchants," which Ford once described as "more than anything a swathe of equable climate rather than a geographical delimitation, a swathe of fertile land rather than a matter of races. It is above all a belt of the world in which men tend to be distinguished by equanimity of mind, frugality, and moderation rather than by huge appetites, crowd massacres, and efficiency."[34] It is this civilization and the temperament of mind it

34. *Great Trade Route*, p. 30.

creates that Ford felt had produced that new breed gradually moving over the face of London; and Fleight is the prototype of this mentality.

It must be remembered that to Ford "race" was always a matter of temperament and environment, the temperament being born of the environment, except in those rare survivals of pure blood strains like Mr. Blood, whose ancestors too took their mood from their surroundings, but centuries earlier. For the remainder of the population, said Ford, "there is in it hardly a man who can point to seven generations of purely English blood, it is almost absurd to use the almost obsolescent word 'race.'" [35] Blood is of course just such a pure type but Fleight is not; he, like Grimshaw of *A Call* and Don Kelleg of *An English Girl,* is a hybrid, born of a Scotch mother and Jewish father. In fact, the society of this novel seems completely peopled with racial hybrids, their very names suggesting the sort of racial interfusion so absorbing to Edwardian sociologists and ethnologists: Wilhelmina Macphail and her sister Augusta with their mixed German-Scots ancestry; Fleight, the Scottish Jew; the young dilettante Cluny Macpherson with "his almond eyes, and his Irish features," who nevertheless turns out to be "half-Armenian, half-Greek."

By contrast with the heterogeneous mixture of modern society, stands Blood with his antediluvian attitude, physique, and temperament, a pure strain which really belongs to a more ebullient past. He may represent as well that attitude of ferocity momentarily displayed in the faltering days of the Empire, what Ford fervently hoped was no more than an Indian-summer phenomenon. And Blood's days, at least in the novel, seem to be numbered, and he is forced to recognize the advantage Fleight's mixed ancestry gives him in a social environment so constituted, a Darwinian dexterity in adapting to the demands of social selection. At a crucial point in the novel, Blood, with characteristic and aristocratic arrogance, puts

35. *England and the English,* p. 264.

Fleight through a little catechism explaining why he, Fleight, is coming to be the representative type even as Blood's day has become a thing of the past:

"And if," Mr. Fleight continued seriously, "You're a Londoner—a cosmopolite—and come from some place where there are real people, pure types . . . it will really handicap you for a Londoner because you will still retain characteristics that will hamper you. But if you come as a sort of hybrid from a couple of races that don't really matter, like Greeks and Armenians . . . you'll just be . . . the typical Englishman of today. . . ."
"And that," Mr. Blood confirmed him, "is why this country is rotting away." [p. 226]

Such evolutionary genetics as Blood drills into Fleight here had widespread support among learned and unlearned alike in the late-Victorian and Edwardian years, men quite ready to argue that the weakening fibre of Western society was undoubtedly traceable to unchecked racial intermixture. From the middle of the nineteenth century onward, there had been a growing school of continental racial theorists, building speciously on Darwin, which insisted that the decline of European civilization itself was linked to the contamination of that original Germanic stock from whence all cultural progress had come. For the majority of these theorists it was the rise to prominence of the Jew that marked the coming dissolution. The conspicuous growth of Jewish financiers, bankers, and brewers, many of whom attained peerages, excited both comment and controversy from social commentators, one of whom went so far as to reprove the king himself for lending the dignity of the crown to his Jewish acquaintances.

In his *Essais sur l' inegalitie des races humaines* (1853), Arthur de Gobineau, assuming the existence of superior and inferior races, had argued a progressive decline of the Germanic racial genius as a result of intermarriage with inferior racial stock. The result, he argued, was observable in the gradual crumbling of European civilization. Symptomatic of that decay was the disappearance of the heroic individualism of a blood nobility, admittedly cruel and brutal, stretching back to the feudal period and a corresponding growth in egalitarian democracy since that time. Blood, by the end of the novel, has emerged as a perfect Gobinist, which is not to argue that Ford had any firsthand knowledge of de Gobineau; but it is not necessary that Ford should have to have been aware of the general outlines of the French ethnologist's ideas.

Working from premises established by de Gobineau and after him G. V. de Lapouge, the great reconciler of Darwinian natural selection and racial evolution, it was Houston Stewart Chamberlain, racial theorist, novelist, and essayist, who gave to his fellow Englishmen a complete summary of European racial speculation. A Cassandra among the Gentiles, he warned of the encroachment of this alien race so unlike our own in temperament and genius: "This alien people has become precisely in the course of the nineteenth century a disproportionately important and on many spheres actually a dominant constituent of our lives." [36] What makes this invasion especially insidious and dangerous, continues Chamberlain, is that "the Jewish people is and remains in Europe an Asiatic people alien to our part of the world, bound to that old law which it received in a distant climate, and which according to its own confession it cannot do away with." [37] Chamberlain here simply follows Herder, who insisted on the essentially alien nature of the Jew, as does Reginald Blood in the novel.

What Chamberlain gave to an entire generation of English readers, as Ernest Sellière [38] has pointed out, was a subtle fusion of Gobinism and Schopenhauerism, which made it but a short step to the Pan-Germanist's assumption of a divine and biological right behind the Teutonic myth of progress and eventual world domination. Chamberlain's theme of race superiority lent support to the

36. Houston Stewart Chamberlain, *Foundations of the Nineteenth Century* (New York, 1912), I, 330.
37. *Ibid.*
38. Ernest Sellière, *Houston-Stewart Chamberlain, Les plus recent philosophe du Pangermanisme mystique* (Paris, 1917).

worst possible expressions of racism and nationalism, both on the continent and in England, where Teutonic cultists found eager enthusiasts among British imperialists, even those of non-Germanic origins. Ford's lifelong contempt for this mentality is scattered throughout his reminiscences, concentrated in his wartime propaganda, and heavily implicit in the conflict of attitudes he dramatizes in *Mr. Fleight*, where it became a part of his theory of psychological progression in the English national spirit.

Any argument for the direct influence of contemporary racial theorists on Ford's social criticism will have to await more positive evidence than is available at present; but the high incidence of similarity, particularly to the theories of Lapouge, suggests Ford's peripheral awareness of racial assumptions, however naive and popularized, as a major aspect of Edwardian social criticism, and as a passionate and Kiplingesque justification for late Imperial designs.

*Mr. Fleight* reflects Ford's continuing search for an effective alien persona from which the Edwardian scene might be viewed in a manner both critical and objective, thus satisfying both Ford's social concern and the canons of his impressionistic art. In a sense the novel has two protagonists who function in this manner—one reflecting the values and perspective of a time long past and whose traditions are now dying out in England; the other embodying the values and abilities of England's coming national spirit. Between the two is caught the patternless flux of an age in transition, with Ford's eternal conflict of tradition and progress.

Mr. Blood, that "last mastodon" of a now extinct historical age, is one of Ford's typically isolated human relics, a once-dominant type that remains now a vestigial survivor in a changing and unfamiliar present. Across the Thames to the east stands Aaron Rothweil Fleight, the coming dominant type. Though he appeals to the psychology, and electorate, of the new age, he nevertheless stands above its anarchic disorders, embodying a compassion, a proficiency, and a communalistic sense all lacking in the Edwardian tangle. His Mediterranean and Hebraic strain has been singled out, through

Ford's process of social selection, from that diversity of England's racial stock that has always assured her "individuals most fitted to deal with the peculiar circumstances of that age." [39] And it was in the closing lines of *England and the English* that Ford had first chosen the Aaron symbol of leadership to suggest England's continuing dominance into the foreseeable future: "For, if this people be not the chosen people, this land will be always one that every race would choose for its birthings and its buryings until the last Aaron shall lead the last of the conquering legions across the world." [40]

Though it far transcends Ford's earlier novels of the contemporary scene, *Mr. Fleight* is the last work in which his social criticism, rendered through the eyes of the alien protagonist, is at all explicitly set forth. And indeed the technique was here almost perfectly muted to Ford's impressionistic aims, but not quite. Total achievement was but one novel away—in *The Good Soldier*. Here Ford would present those same symptoms of individual deterioration and civilization's decay but with his underlying historical thesis fully absorbed into the narrative web of that sad story.

39. Ford, *England and the English*, p. 278.
40. *Ibid.*, p. 354.

# 6. The Good Soldier

"... *it is a tale*
*Told by an idiot, full of sound and fury,*
*Signifying nothing.*"

At once so like and unlike anything he had written up to that time, Ford's *The Good Soldier* represents both a reversal and a continuation of theme and techniques that had been growing for over a dozen years. The novel is easily his fullest, most convincing portrait of a valueless and anarchic present busily shoring up its ruins, while destroying those few worthwhile humans left to wander across its landscape. A full and accurate account of the sources Ford drew upon is only gradually becoming apparent; and the failure of early critics to fully suggest the book's antecedents is probably traceable to two facts: one, the dazzling pyrotechnics of the novel inevitably shoulder aside other considerations when it is first read and, two, Ford's own comments on the book have confused as much as clarified. He liked to insist that his "great Auk's egg," as he once termed it, had sprung, Minerva-like, full-blown from his head—an exciting prospect, but totally untrue.

What is clear is that both the ostensible germ of the plot, as well as the historical explanation of Edward Ashburnham's plight, come from *England and the English*, begun a decade earlier. Ford's anecdote of the countryman and his ward who inspired the outlines of the plot has been told and retold a sufficient number of times to preclude the necessity for repeating the story here. And Ford's historical outline of England's past in the same book has already been described in detail. In both theme and technique, but most particularly in its consummate use of the alien persona, *The Good Soldier* became the perfect and watertight vehicle for Ford's social and historical diagnostics.

The appropriateness of the novel's point of view lay in the fact that although Ford resorts to the immediate narrative voice, all signs of authorship are obliterated from the novel. From this emerged that artful irony that henceforth the character of the teller might loom as large in motive and psychology as in any Browning monologue without in any way detracting from impressionistic aims. The employment of the teller's idiosyncratic voice signals Ford's movement away from the severely detached narrative voice of the earlier novels, a voice that had too often been compelled finally to resort to some more or less omniscient character to clarify themes. There had been repeated signs of such movement in *Ladies Whose Bright Eyes* and *Mr. Fleight;* but the swiftness and authority with which Ford moved into the new mode remains one of the most amazing leaps in his development.

In later years, though he was writing after the fact, Ford recalled his and Conrad's continuing attempt to hypnotize the reader into that willing suspension of disbelief: "We wanted the readers to forget the writers, to forget that he was reading. We wished him to be hypnotized into thinking that he was living what he read—or, at least, into the conviction that he was listening to a simple and in no

ay brilliant narrator who was telling—not writing—a true story." [1]
nquestionably Ford's naturally expansive and anecdotal mind
)und first-person narrative a thoroughly congenial mode and, in
)hn Dowell, that "simple and in no way brilliant narrator" he and
:onrad had sought, each in ways peculiar to himself. " 'As for me,'
ord wrote some years later, 'I went on working beside Conrad,
trying . . . to evolve for myself a vernacular of an extreme quiet-
ness that would suggest some one of refinement talking in a low
voice near the ear of someone he liked a good deal.' " [2] And it
was in this low-keyed, Browningesque voice that Ford was to spin
his finest tale, built around the life and actions of his most recurrent
figure, the alien protagonist.

In terms of the figure whose development we have been tracing,
the most arresting difference between *Mr. Fleight* and *The Good
Soldier* is the increasing somberness of outlook in the latter novel.
At last, momentarily Ford was suggesting in *Mr. Fleight* that there
might still be a place in the world for the sort of virtues exemplified
by the alien protagonist of that novel. Within two years all such
optimism had disappeared from *The Good Soldier*. Where *Mr.
Fleight* was concerned with the coming ascendancy of a new dominant type, *The Good Soldier* concentrates—once again—on the fate
of the old, the man who stands for a world order long since
dissolved into the past. And where *Mr. Fleight* had shown a hopefulness that the coming type would represent a return to a national
spirit of compassion and community, summed up in Fleight's Mediterranean-feudal heritage, *The Good Soldier* reflects by contrast the
gradual emergence and dominance of unprincipled and uncompassionate figures like Leonora Ashburnham and Dowell, whose temperamental coldness and unconcern with traditional values suggests
that of the Dimensionists of *The Inheritors*. In a way they are the
direct lineal descendants of those allegorical symbols for the post–

1. Ford Madox Ford, *Return to Yesterday* (New York, 1932), pp. 216–17.
2. Ford Madox Ford, *Mightier than the Sword* (London, 1938), p. 378.

Boer War mentality, though they are conceived not in terms of Wellsian fantasy but of Ford's historical mythos. These figures, through an evolutionary process of social and historical selection, are replacing older types like Ashburnham with his feudal heritage of passion, idealism, and aristocratic responsibility—but most of all that clarity of moral vision lost to the Age of Relativity.

In this apparently artless tale, told in the easy and disarming vernacular of a recording mind whose psychological distortions reflect its sick milieu, comes the halting story of two couples: the John Dowells and the Edward Ashburnhams. Of the foursome, only three are initially important to narrative action: Edward Ashburnham, his wife Leonora, and Florence Dowell. On the periphery of their relationship is John Dowell, the otiose and deferential husband of Florence, whose mind becomes the staging area for all subsequent action. Moving with insensate routine, he picks his way through deceitful and self-flattering corridors of memory, piecing together the now-shattered relationships of their life. His simplistic world of values and sense of human relationships devastated by the discovery of his wife's adulterous affairs, Dowell speaks to the reader out of his confusion and doubt as the novel opens. The leveling of Dowell's value structures, the moral wasteland now spreading before him, these become the desolate stage upon which Ford sets going his usual representatives of Time Past and Time Present. His objective, as always, was to show his present generation where it stood in that long evolutionary development of the English national spirit. Whether or not he felt the world view embodied in Ashburnham was any longer a viable alternative to the collapse of Western culture, it was at least a reminder of what had been lost along the way.

The character of Ashburnham is the most subtly conceived of all Ford's disjunctive protagonists wrenched from their proper time slots, a man of honor whose vestigial sentiments and lapsed values have no place in the modern world, and whose death in that world gives pause to the whole concept of Progress. And the antecedents

f Ashburnham's values, despite his dislocation in time, are as ob-
iously medieval as those of Katherine Howard of the historical
ovels or Mr. Blood of the contemporary.

The perfection of the alien protagonist provided the consummate
olution to the problem of the Impressionist who, on the Edwardian
cene, was assuming the role of social historian to the age. Pledged to
do nothing more than "render" the world as he saw it, Ford represents the English wing of the Zolaesque tradition that had argued,
"We do not have to draw a conclusion from our works . . . our
works carry their conclusion with them." [3] Consequently critics
who argue, as Kenner has done, that "the narrator's bewilderment is
Ford's most serviceable device; for it prevents him from having to
resolve the book" [4] are really tilting at windmills of their own
creation. The very absence of any resolution to the dilemma presented in the novel constitutes its final commentary, an open-ended-
ness that was rapidly becoming the vogue in both Edwardian drama
and fiction, for—as one character in the novel puts it—"the whole
thing just goes on and on."

Ford the Impressionist was determined not to falsify or simplify
the bewildering complexity of the Edwardian scene by suggesting
any easy solution of its problems. The most he would do was to
render it as objectively as possible, turning it this way and that in
the light of the novelist's imagination. A passage from *Mightier than
the Sword*, written twenty years later, shows that Ford found no
occasion to change his mind in later life, although then, as earlier, he
had no objection to framing the world's events within some meaningful pattern:

For it is characteristic of a confused world . . . that along with the disappearance of Continence, Probity, and the belief in revealed religion,
Truth should have developed the bewildering faculty of the chameleon

3. Emile Zola, *The Experimental Novel*, trans. Belle M. Sherman (New
York, 1893), p. 30.
4. Hugh Kenner, "Conrad and Ford: The Artistic Conscience," *Shenandoah*,
III (Summer, 1952), p. 54.

and have taken on like Janus, two faces. . . . So the novelist—the authentic and valid novelist whose duty it is to record his world in crystallized form so that it may be of advantage to posterity—the novelist seeing both sides of Truth can do no more than take one side at one moment and the other immediately afterwards.[5]

Fortunately the novelist is less chary of handling big words like *Truth, Meaning,* and *Purpose* than the philosopher; and these are what *The Good Soldier* is all about.

The central issue of the novel, voiced through Dowell's periodic questioning, is that of purpose, meaning, and pattern in an age of relative values. As Dowell puts it in that central image upon which the novel opens: "If for nine years I have possessed a goodly apple that is rotten at the core and discover its rottenness only in nine years and six months less four days, isn't it true to say that for nine years I possessed a goodly apple? So it may well be with Edward Ashburnham, with Leonora his wife and with poor dear Florence." (p. 18) Later Dowell repeatedly protests the pointlessness of those events that destroy both couples' marriages, drive Nancy mad, Edward and Florence to suicide, and Leonora into a loveless marriage, leaving Dowell the role of joyless caretaker over the rubble of their common past. Again and again Dowell strews these questions in the reader's path: "Why did things work out as they did? For what purpose? To point what lesson? It is all a darkness." Nor is Dowell indulging his love of self-dramatization when he describes his role as narrator as that of a scribe to his age, one who has "witnessed the sack of a city or the falling to pieces of a people"; for the collapse Ford shows us through his eyes is not that of a family, a small circle, or even a class. It is the decline of English society itself, even as he had fearfully predicted it in *England and the English,* and as he had unsuccessfully symbolized it in *The Inheritors,* but now realized through perfectly believable, convincingly individualized characters. And always in the background is the unmistakable rumble of Ford's historical machinery.

5. *Mightier than the Sword,* p. 235.

Never amidst that continual and unremitting intensification of action, pain, and suffering does Dowell ever suggest that the root cause of the misfortunes may lie with that destiny, "august and inscrutable," that was part of Ford's own superstitious cast. Instead, Dowell says of these events: "It is so sad, just because there was no current to draw things along to a swift and inevitable end." Later in the novel, he suggests that there was "no nemesis, no destiny" driving them before it. But the underlying pattern is there nevertheless, glimpsed even by Dowell in one late and crucial scene, a pattern of historical conflict and tragedy stretching nearly unbroken from *The Fifth Queen* to *The Good Soldier.*

The forces that destroy Ashburnham are those abroad in all Ford's novels of the contemporary scene: secularism, materialism, and their inevitable concomitant—the breakdown of all human relationships. The defeat of Ashburnham before the combined forces of modern dissolution was a reiteration of Ford's most persistent complaint, that who of his father, as well as Green and Conrad: that Time and Progress in their secular hurry made no provision for the preservation of splendid and unusual types. They are, in fact, inevitably discarded because the new Time Spirit in no way requires them.

Ford's last attempt at his medieval ideal, Ashburnham is less starkly recognizable than, say, Norfolk of the Tudor novels, though he retains the old, out-of-doors physiognomy that had typified the older type in his ruddiness of complexion. His eyes, like theirs, are "perfectly honest, perfectly straightforward," not the devious, twinkling eyes of the Tudor Machiavellians. By contrast with the sexually diffident Dowell, like Leonora a cold and cerebral modern, Ashburnham has the passions, vigor, and energy of the medieval dominant type. Like them he becomes uneasy when confronted by the necessity for reflection. "Having too much in one's head," as he once puts it, "would really interfere with one's quickness" (p. 44). But these physical characteristics of Ford's medieval type are of less moment than those extinct notions of honor and duty that are built into Ashburnham's character, notions as antithetical to the men of his day as the passions he can only feel as a shortcoming in himself: "Along with Edward's passions and his shame for them went the violent conviction of the duties of his station" (p. 59). The adjective "violent" is, of course, Dowell's, for whom any expression of conviction must seem extreme, lacking as he does Edward's vigor and sense of *noblesse oblige*.

A latter-day feudalist, Ashburnham has that active sense of communal responsibility and aristocratic leadership that Robert Grimshaw saw crumbling in twentieth-century England. While this might seem a somewhat tardy awareness of feudalism's decline, it had become an increasingly popular economic argument in Ford's day, accepted in the highest quarters of government, and by Ford's close friend Masterman in particular. Writing of the rapid disappearance of the great country estates, Masterman warned of their passing as one more symptom of England's decay: "And such appears, to some at least, to be the condition today of ancient systems, whose stability at the present receives scarcely a passing challenge. The first, and perhaps the most far-reaching of these, is the English Landed System: the feudal organization, with all its implications of leadership and obedience, as embedded in the very heart of the old life of England." [6] And following that system into decay, Masterman continued, were those men—like Edward Ashburnham—who had presided over it: "the . . . country gentleman, the type of the lesser landed aristocracy of England, is already becoming a thing of the past." [7] Consequently Ford's association of contemporary social decline with the disappearance of the old landed estates was really one of the economic truisms of the day and no idiosyncratic notion born of his historical theories, but Ford does make Ashburnham's failure the result of his grandiose and slightly ambiguous vision of English history. Ashburnham's destruction is at once the tragedy of a man, of a type, of an entire culture—that perfect fusion of the

6. C. F. G. Masterman, *In Peril of Change* (New York, n.d.), p. 119.
7. *Ibid.*, p. 311

historical and the personal that is the highest achievement of *The Good Soldier*. Ashburnham represents the tail end of a tradition already seen threatened by the old Duke of Norfolk in *The Fifth Queen*.

An unwilling member in that lost tribe of feudal country gentlemen, cut off from any vital past, and drifting from one European spa to another, Ashburnham with his troubled sense of feudal responsibility seems to one of the new men like Dowell little more than a Quixotic sentimentalist, with those odd little tastes and mannerisms that set him apart from the men of his day. Though of Anglican stock, he feels that strange compulsive sympathy for Roman Catholicism with its ritual emphasis and traditionally collective spirit. And there is his peculiar passion for the chronicles of Froissart (a favorite of Ford's own), as well as the novels of Walter Scott, whose out-of-fashion heroes he often resembles. Both his tastes and his temperament lean back into the past. Most troublesome to those around him as well as to critics is his supposedly ambivalent personality. Whether or not Ashburnham is to be regarded as a totally admirable figure has been a puzzle and a trouble to critics, most of whom prefer to see him as the archetype of the nonhero of modern fiction—a man with weaknesses as well as virtues and therefore acceptable to the post-Freudian reader. Even the most astute of Ford critics, Paul Wiley, sees Ashburnham as the modern ur-hero, one seen "in the double focus of hero and bungler." [8] Elliott Gose, on the other hand, singles out two Ashburnhams, in arguing the psychological complexity of his character: "On the one hand there is what we may call the internal Edward, driven 'by the mad passion to find an ultimately satisfying woman.' On the other hand there is the external Ashburnham, 'the fine soldier, the excellent landlord, the extraordinarily kind, careful, and industrious magistrate, the upright, honest, fair-dealing, fair-thinking, public character.' " [9]

8. Paul Wiley, *Novelist of Three Worlds: Ford Madox Ford* (Syracuse, N.Y., 1962), p. 190.

9. Elliott B. Gose, "The Strange Irregular Rhythm: An Analysis of *The Good Soldier*," *PMLA*, LXXII (June, 1957), 497.

All such psychological analysis of Ashburnham as a personality divided against itself ignores Ford's conception of what the medieval temperament was like. Ford had already experimented with the sort of mild schizophrenia one finds in Robert Grimshaw, but it was no part of his plan in *The Good Soldier*. If there is any conflict *within* Ashburnham, it is not that of the divided nature warring against itself. Psychologically he is *tout ensemble*, all of a piece—but it was a piece made for the world of six hundred years ago. Within Ford's medieval type there was no sense of contradiction between his idealism and altruism on the one hand and his unbridled passions, in love and war, on the other—only an earlier age's recognition of that sweet anarchy of the body, functioning as best it could under a demanding but forgiving God. Ashburnham's medieval passions are meant to contrast starkly with that modern paralysis born of social restraint that leads to those eruptions of maddened Nordicism Ford was suggesting in Grimshaw of *A Call* and attributed generally to the north European mentality in *Great Trade Route*. As such it is part of that modern malady that infects "good people," like Leonora Ashburnham, driving them through sexual repression to those small and persistent acts of cruelty and persecution that proliferate towards the close of *The Good Soldier*.

Edward, of course, is himself troubled for the same reason as the critics. Neither understands the plight he is placed in—a medieval psychological type at variance with the modern types around him. Consequently he seems admirable to modern critics only in a qualified way. They approve his sense of honor and duty but are troubled by his ungovernable passions. Yet this is to judge him solely by modern standards, the same error historians make currently in following the new vogue for reconstructing historical figures out of the past in terms of modern psychology. Placed in a medieval context Ashburnham requires no apology for the coexistence of passion and idealism in his makeup. What other example is needed to demonstrate the medieval fusion of passion and idealism than a sense of honor that compels him to give up Nancy—the very object of those same high passions!

If there was any qualification in Ford's own admiration for Ashburnham, it was only because he realized that such a type was no longer feasible by modern standards, and would inevitably be viewed as "sentimental"—Dowell's favorite term—in an age that has neither use nor understanding of his values, which are, after all, as Gose points out, those of "a feudal gentleman." [10] Obviously feudal gentlemen can hardly manage to survive in a modern world where, as Ford once wrote, "the feudal system in its perfection has died out. . . ." [11] Ashburnham's misfortune is directly traceable to Ford's historical wheel of fortune which decrees that although the age in which his type reached pre-eminence has long since passed, he and others like him occasionally persist beyond their age of domination. Admirable as a vestigial survivor who embodied Ford's personal feudal ideal, Ashburnham provided Ford with a symbol of a once stable and meaningful society against which to contrast those modern forces of cultural anarchy. Ashburnham's suicide in the novel is simply the climactic and symbolic expression of those inexorable forces of historical and social selection that ruthlessly weed out anachronisms such as he and Nancy. A grim view of the world, and perfectly Conradesque, Henry Hudson of *The "Half-Moon"* had seen the sacrifice of such men as a part of ineluctable process. And it was the same philosophic conviction that Ford, if he did not hear it from his father's lips, certainly read from the elder Hueffer's pen: that bleak determinism that drives forward both men and the universe "at the cost of inconceivable individual suffering [and] creates new types only to abandon them again to the universal doom of destruction." [12]

Little wonder that Ford, the young student at Praetoria House, should have fallen under the lifelong influence of Green's *Short History*, with its evolutionary explanation of English history as a

10. *Ibid.*
11. Ford Madox Ford, *Henry James: A Critical Study* (New York, 1964), p. 47.
12. Francis Hueffer, *Musical Studies* (Edinburgh, 1880), p. 122.

continual progression of English national psychology embodied in historical figures who, as Emery Neff describes it in *The Poetry of History,* "represent and embody social manifestations."[13] Nor is it any more surprisng that Green's highly dramatic handling of his material should have given Ford many of the scenes and dialogues of the early historical novels, in addition to Ford's ruling theory of history which underlies the deterministic failure of so many of his alien protagonists. And there is that same sense of irrevocable process at work behind the scenes of *The Good Soldier,* despite Dowell's disclaimer that "there was no current to draw things along to a swift and inevitable end . . . there is about it no nemesis, no destiny" (p. 146). The whole tenor of the novel argues against Dowell's rejection of some dark fate; and we realize that in Dowell's characteristic misunderstanding we have another of those refracted truths in which the novel abounds. By the end of the novel even Dowell comes to a surer understanding of those dim forces, blind and inexorable, behind the Ashburnham tragedy, forces that were the mainspring of Ford's historical theory: "Conventions and traditions, I suppose, work blindly but surely for the preservation of the normal type; for the extinction of proud, resolute, and unusual individuals. . . . So Edward and Nancy found themselves steamrolled out and Leonora survives, the perfectly normal type. . . . So those splendid and tumultuous creatures with their magnetism and their passions . . . have gone from this earth." (p. 205)

And with their splendor, passions, and vigor went Ford's feudal ideal, giving way before the new dominant type embodied in figures like Leonora, Dowell, and Rodney Bayham who are neither proud, nor resolute, nor individuals. Of Bayham all we know is that all of his clothes could be "bought ready-made." The tragedy implicit in Ford's view of history is that those types best suited to survive in the world, Nature's choice as it were, are those which least command our respect and admiration—even as Thomas Huxley had warned

13. Emery Neff, *The Poetry of History* (New York, 1947), pp. 183–84.

long before. If the prospect was a bleak one, it was, nevertheless, Ford's final summing up, on the eve of the Great War, of the direction taken by Western man in the twentieth century.

Gradually Ford learned to adjust his deterministic scheme to either the environmental factor, such as Zola used, or to Flaubertian emphasis on temperament. As causal forces in human action, the two are easily interchangeable, the environmental factor being but the reverse of the temperamental side of the coin—as is the case in *The Good Soldier*, where Ashburnham's temperament results from a familial tradition reaching back to another time and place. Clearly Ford's handling of his historical *apparat* was more effective in the historical novels than in his first novels dealing with the contemporary scene. Part of the reason lies in the response the historical novel elicits from the reader. Our ideas of the past have settled down into a few fixed notions which can then be read into characters and situations; but it is far more difficult to have any substantive knowledge, even a free and generalized one, of our own age, particularly if, like the Edwardian period, it is experiencing a sweeping revolution in manners and morals. If it is difficult to see clearly through the dark glass of the present, it is even more difficult to render what lies there—which the Impressionist seeks to do—in terms of fiction. This problem, as I have suggested earlier, drove Ford, along with others, to superimpose some sort of conceptual grid on the pattern of world events.

The partial failure of Ford's earlier novels based in a modern setting—novels like *An English Girl* and *A Call*—stemmed from his failure to embody convincingly the Time Spirit of the Edwardian Age against which men like Don Kelleg and Robert Grimshaw ineffectually struggle. In *The Good Soldier* this weakness has almost disappeared. Instead of pitting his alien protagonist against a nebulous "spirit of the age," insufficiently dramatized in some major antagonist, Ford created in one pre-eminently believable adversary, Leonora Ashburnham, a character who combined the multitude of modern tendencies Ford felt to be a contravention of his feudal ideal. A modern day Erinys, Leonora obsessively tortures her husband into despair and suicide, partly through the sexual perversity of an Anne Jeal or Sylvia Tietjens, but also because of a maddening inability to understand her husband and the impossible ideals motivating him. Though she desires him physically, she is bewildered, even infuriated by his feudal sense of responsibility to the family estate and tenantry, which threatens the financial security she prizes above all things. Conversely, he can say he "admires her tremendously," but he is incapable of really understanding or taking seriously her modern, and to Ford "Nordic," sense of efficiency and fiscal responsibility. Unfortunately she cannot inspire in him, for those same reasons, those natural passions of which she knows him capable with other, less efficient women.

As husband and wife the two are fatefully mismated, representing as they do medieval and modern psychological types thrown willy-nilly together by that late-Victorian custom of arranged marriages. Where he is idealistic and sentimental, she is practical and materialistic. Born of an English family already uprooted from its native soil, brought up in an unfamiliar Irish countryside by a family in uneasy financial circumstances, Leonora can understand nothing of Edward's mad attachment to the land of his ancestors nor the principle of feudal interdependency he adheres to. His openhanded generosity drives her to despair as the acts of an irresponsible and sentimental idealist. And by contrast with Edward's passionate feudal nature there is about Leonora that constant suggestion of coldness of which even the impercipient Dowell, the other sterile modern, is at times aware: "I seemed to feel when I looked at them [Leonora's shoulders] that, if ever I should press my lips upon them that they would be slightly cold. . . . I seemed to feel chilled at the end of my lips when I looked at her. . . ." (p. 38) Leonora's cold and unfeminine nature is totally incapable of arousing in Edward those feudal passions all too ready to erupt over frail, feminine natures like Maisie Maidan and Nancy Rufford, even over the predatory Florence, who has her own mindless and acquiescent appeal.

But there is more than a temperamental opposition, a sort of Flaubertian determinism, driving these two towards ruin. There are additional barriers of religion and ancestry. A spiritually austere and convent-reared Roman Catholic, Leonora fails utterly to understand her husband's lightly held Anglicanism nor his apparently carefree indifference to moral strictures. Although Ford seems to be denying those very feudal-Catholic, modern-Protestant alignments he outlined in his historical system, such is not the case. Ford was obviously associating the cold and individualistic Leonora with the bleak austerity of the Puritan conscience, born of Calvin and Knox and now fastened absolutely upon the English national spirit, as indeed it was upon most of northern Europe. This peculiar phenomenon Ford was to describe later in *Great Trade Route*, in pointing out the influence of national temperament in evolving different Catholic types: "Catholicism of course differs widely and evolves national types in every nation. But, for Catholics at least, it is everywhere distinguished by one thing . . . by, precisely, a sort of gaiety." [14] Leonora is but nominally a Catholic, not temperamentally as is, paradoxically, Edward, who, despite his Anglican upbringing, is emotionally drawn towards her faith, considering at one point in the novel becoming a convert.

The religious difference between the two, however, is but a corollary to that essential antagonism of modern and feudal temperament, each born of its historical age. Working on her own ground and within her own milieu, Leonora is recognizable and understandable as the modern type, but Edward exists here, amidst an alien landscape, only as the tail end of a tradition. Consequently Ford was at pains to suggest that the roots of Ashburnham's lineage reach back to the great barons, as his family name is meant to suggest. There is but the briefest mention in the novel of Edward's having been descended "from the Ashburnham who accompanied Charles I

14. Ford Madox Ford, *Great Trade Route* (New York and Toronto, 1937), p. 388.

to the scaffold" (p. 16). Behind this terse biography was the longer history of the Ashburnham family, which Ford had described in his historical and descriptive work *The Cinque Ports* (1900). The Cinque Ports in Ford's mind represented one of the last strongholds of the old medieval barony; and the Brothers of the Cinque Ports the last of the feudal barons, placing Edward Ashburnham in that same feudal line represented by Edward Colman of *The "Half-Moon."*

Through details such as these Ford creates that sense of fated conflict born of irreconcilable differences in character, ancestry, and circumstances which lead Edward and Leonora Ashburnham to their inevitable and tragic end. As such *The Good Soldier* achieved Ford's ultimate aim in fiction: a sense of inevitable destiny which presides over the lives of so many of his characters. In Leonora's progressive ascendancy over her husband, Ford has dramatized, in a pair of lives, the triumph of an unprincipled and morally anarchic Time Spirit over an older tradition built on honor, probity, and a sense of communal interdependence. The difference in the psychological nature of antagonist and alien protagonist is the difference between the dissident, individualistic and fragmented modern temperament and that of a feudal society whose positive values arise from that solid interlacing of the secular and religious: "And he [Edward] was beginning to perceive dimly that, whereas his own traditions were entirely collective, his wife was a sheer individualist. His own theory—the feudal theory of an over-lord doing his best by his dependents, the dependents meanwhile doing their best for the over-lord—this theory was entirely foreign to Leonora's nature." (p. 132) And the theory, Edward might have gone on, is equally foreign to the whole of modern society.

The same forces of historical determinism that had destroyed Katherine Howard and Edward Colman and crippled Don Kelleg and Robert Grimshaw are those underlying the failure of Edward Ashburnham, the finest impressionistic rendering of Ford's most recurrent figure: the idealist whose virtues and values are not of the time or place into which he is born. His alien persona was, again, that coign of vantage from which Ford mounted his criticism of the contemporary scene.

During the decade from 1905 to 1915 Ford sought to present an unbiased account of his age within some comprehensible, if unseen, framework of history. To dramatize a demoralized and schismatic present to an audience that took these things for granted, it was necessary to locate some place in history an alternative ideal of human behavior. Unquestionably it was Ford's personal as well as artistic need that led him to that comprehensive theory of historical development, a scheme wherein even the bewildering flux of Edwardian England could be seen as part of some larger design. Such a scheme need not be literally true if it gave him a fixed point by which to organize his impressions into some meaningful pattern, "some convenient system of thought by which a man may arrange in his mind his mental image of the mundane cosmogony." Nowhere did Ford suggest that this private teleology was anything other than the sort of imaginative projection to which the modern artist was of necessity driven, one that provided him with a closed system of values from which to operate and to draw his metaphors.

# Index